ANTHON[...]

PHOENIX FLIGHT MANUAL

...Rising Above The Ashes of Ordinary Existence

THREE BLUE HERONS PUBLISHING, INC.

PHOENIX FLIGHT MANUAL

...Rising Above The Ashes of Ordinary Existence

Copyright 1995
Anthony S. Dallmann-Jones, Ph.D.

ISBN # 1-881952-49-5

No part of this publication may be reproduced, stored in or introduced into a retrieval system, or transmitted in any form, or by any means, without the prior written permission of the copyright owner.

Cover art by ZAK

THREE BLUE HERONS PUBLISHING, INC.
P.O. Box 463, Fond du Lac, WI 54936-0463

**Dedicated to
the personal empowerment
potential in each of us.**

Sometimes you find happiness along the road of life by mere chance. The greatest magical truth one can discover is that sustained happiness is a skill that can be learned.

ACKNOWLEDGEMENTS

It is a delight to acknowledge the explorers of the frontiers of consciousness listed in the Bibliography. They have written of their adventures that we might learn. I am overwhelmed by their sheer brilliance and perseverance. Emotions arise in me as I look over their names, privileged to work among these flowers of courage and curiosity in the meadows of the human potential movement.

I acknowledge my friends, colleagues, and students who have endured my research, brainstorming, preoccupation, and contagious enthusiasm as I developed this manual.

I thank my consultant and advisor, Simon Warwick-Smith, for his invaluable insight, advice, efforts, and *bloody* sense of humor in bringing the *PHOENIX FLIGHT MANUAL* to the marketplace. I also thank LuAn, Janis, Karl, Robert, Gary and Kathy for their valuable support and assistance.

I acknowledge my wife, Amy, for her encouragement, support, and editorial assistance. It is my good fortune to be in love with such an intelligent, beautiful, helpful and spiritual woman.

I especially acknowledge the human spirit in all of us, the spirit that quests on and on.

FOREWORD

Ours is a busy world. People need things that work well and work quickly. The distance between scientific discovery and everyday application has always been frustrating. The purpose of this book is to introduce in practical form the most advanced independent technique for self-actualizing ever developed. I call this psychological breakthrough *The Phoenix Solution*. It will work for you. It will put you so firmly and positively in the driver's seat of your life that you will forget what it was like to be powerless.

Anthony S. Dallmann-Jones, Ph.D.
Fond du Lac, Wisconsin

TABLE OF CONTENTS

Part One - User's Manual

INTRODUCTION   1

CHAPTER 1 -
PSYCHOTECHNOLOGY AND HOW IT WORKS   7
   The Unlimited Power of Psychotechnology...
   The Latest Breakthrough: The Phoenix Solution...

CHAPTER 2 -
EVERY THOUGHT HAS POWER   11
   The Freest People in The World...
   The Source of Power in You...
   To Be Truly Free...
   Four Truths You Can Believe In...
   The Seven Paralyzing Fears...

CHAPTER 3 -
THE PSYCHOTECHNOLOGY SOLUTION   19
   The History of Psychotechnology...
   The Nine Principles...

CHAPTER 4 -
TAKE CHARGE OF YOUR LIFE   33
   Your Locus of Control...
   Limits & Boundaries...
   Power...
   Two Truths You Can Believe In...
   Six Excuses For Staying Powerless...

CHAPTER 5 -
THE COMFORT ZONE   43
   What runs your life...
   Two ways to eliminate friction...

CHAPTER 6 - THE PHOENIX SOLUTION   47
    Introduction...
    The Unity of Experience...
    The Essential Five Steps of The Phoenix Solution...

CHAPTER 7 - THE PHOENIX SOLUTION - STEP 1   53
    Passionately Possessing the Problem...
        A) Emotionally: Willingness - 5 Types
        B) Mentally: Responsibility
        C) Physically: Conscious Connected Breathing
    Seven Truths to Believe In...
    Real Examples...

CHAPTER 8 - THE PHOENIX SOLUTION - STEP 2   71
    Understanding the Problem...
    Six Dynamics of Problems...
    A) Problem Identification: Assessing the Situation...
        3 Blocks to Accurate Assessment You Should Know
    B) Expanding the Number of Possible Explanations...
        The Powerful Listing Method
    C) Selecting the Most Accurate Explanation...
    Five Truths to Believe In...
    Real Examples...

CHAPTER 9 - THE PHOENIX SOLUTION - STEP 3   89
    Formulating the Answer...
    Simplifying the Problem into a Modifier Statement...
    Seven Guidelines for Great Modifiers...
    Shaping the Modifier into a Primary Domino Thought...
    Attaching a Timer...
    Real Examples...

CHAPTER 10 -
THE PHOENIX SOLUTION - STEP 4   99
    Implementation...
    Essential Step 4 Glossary...
    Visualization of Implantation...
        Creating the Good Moment
        Shifting Contexts
        Humor
        Pleasant Memories
    Generating the Emotion of Accomplishment...
    Generating the Physical Sensation of Accomplishment...
    Two Truths You Can Believe In...
    Real Examples...

CHAPTER 11 -
THE PHOENIX SOLUTION - Step 5   115
    Refinement...
    The Step 5 Checklist...
    A Note About Results...
    Real Examples...

CHAPTER 12 -
CONCLUSION TO USER'S MANUAL   121
    The Phoenix Solution Outline...
    Designing Your World...

Part Two - Technical Manual

APPENDIX I   127
    The Map of Modification...
    The Phoenix Solution Ancillary...

INTRODUCTION   129

THE MAP OF MODIFICATION	**129**
AWARENESS	**136**
INTENTION	**139**
PROBLEM LOCATION	**140**
INTERNAL LOCUS OF CONTROL	**143**
THE 9 APPROACHES TO LIFE	**144**
A BRIEF HISTORY OF PSYCHOTECHNOLOGY	**148**
PASSIONATE PROBLEM POSSESSION	**154**
Willingness...	
Responsibility...	
Conscious connected breathing...	
PROBLEM DEVELOPMENT	**161**
Commitment...	
MODIFIER DEVELOPMENT	**169**
Formulation...	
Affirmation guidelines...	
MODIFIER APPLICATION	**175**
Creating good moments...	
Recontextualization...	
Generating accomplishment...	
Imaging...	
Feeling...	
APPENDIX II	**181**
The E.R.P. List...	
APPENDIX III	**191**
Establishing purpose...	
BIBLIOGRAPHY	**197**
ORDER FORM	**203**
INDEX	**205**

INTRODUCTION

Knowing just how much work it is to write a book, it intrigues me to know why the book I am about to read was written. I can best communicate the reason that I have spent years researching, experimenting, writing and rewriting to publish the *Phoenix Flight Manual* by having you do the following exercise: Imagine a friend of yours sitting across from you with 200 packets of nice crisp $100 bills—that's a total of one million dollars. As you sit there, unable to do anything but watch, he/she pours lighter fluid over the stack and sets it on fire for no apparent reason. Imagine being there and helplessly having to watch all that money burn into ashes. How do you feel? Seriously. What a waste, right? Money appears to be just paper, but we know that it is human energy stored in a flat green battery. Our pain in seeing the money burn is actually our experiencing intense regret in watching all that potential going up in flames.

As an educator and psychotherapist for over three decades, I have felt that same feeling of regret many times. I feel that way watching great human potential going to waste. I have watched people enduring pain from day to day believing that they have no other choice. I have watched people giving up their dreams and experiencing endless, meaningless days believing that is all there is to life. I have watched people in constant anxiety, boredom or compulsivity believing there is no hope, and people walking around in trances escaping to a fantasy world where they vicariously live out their lives believing that this is as good as it's going to get.

Frankly, it hurts to watch. It especially hurts to watch when you know there is a powerful effective way out of any and all of those states of mind and being. When you know there is a no-fail way for a person to rise from their own ashes, no matter how far down they have gone, you have no choice but to find a means to communicate it to those who need it. You are holding in your hands that means. If you read this manual and utilize the Phoenix Solution as conveyed to you in its pages, I promise that you will experience success in every applied area.

This book is for people seeking a better way to create and command change in their lives. Change is all about getting from here to there, slowing things down, or speeding things up. To know how to control change is to be *empowered*. To utilize that knowledge is power. A lot of books talk about empowerment, but few books show you how to create and utilize power. This one does.

The magic of Psychotechnology is demonstrated by its amazing outcomes, or *results*. I developed this particular psycho-technological method known as the Phoenix Solution to provide you with *results*. There is nothing like it. Many people have utilized the Phoenix Solution to efficiently attain their goals. These goals have included losing weight, creating mood shifts, healing physical problems, lowering golf scores, quitting smoking, smoothing out relationships, and many other goals people usually find difficult to accomplish. By using the Phoenix Solution your mind becomes your skilled and powerful assistant, allowing you to create *magical* transitions in your life at will. As I said, there is nothing like it.

Note: The usual pattern in the development of self-help knowledge is that first there are scientific breakthroughs made in relative obscurity by researchers. Then the research is written up over a period of time and eventually finds its way into a scientific journal. More obscurity. Then the research is replicated by someone(s) a few years later, and that is published in another scientific journal a few years after that–maybe. Then, perhaps, someone will take the information and begin to translate it into language suitable for the general public. After another few years, the benefits may begin to be realized. This is not the case with the *Phoenix Flight Manual* and Psychotechnology.

Psychotechnology turns this cumbersome process around. Psychotechnology is measured by a number of factors, but the two most important ones are *practicality* and *acceleration,* i.e., it works and it works fast. In keeping with that value system, the *Phoenix Flight Manual* is divided into two parts, communicating to the consumer first and the professional second. Part I, The User's Manual, is about expedient practicality. It gives enough detail and background in everyday language to make the Phoenix Solution meaningful and still easily applicable. Part II is the Technical Manual for those wanting more detail or more jargon or both. Part I is more than sufficient to get you the results you want. This is proven by the fact that the first three field-tested versions of the *Phoenix Flight Manual* did not include the Technical Manual, yet produced all the results you will read about in this volume.

Part One

THE USER'S MANUAL

CHAPTER 1

PSYCHOTECHNOLOGY AND HOW IT WORKS
The Unlimited Power of Psychotechnology
The Latest Breakthrough: The Phoenix Solution

This book's time has come. Ten years ago *psychotechnology* was in its infancy, and the notion of deliberate transformation of the self was but a beautiful dream. Today the Phoenix Solution is the most powerful tool for designer living available. It has helped hundreds of people transform their lives and achieve the future they always wanted but never could attain.

Linda Evans, an executive in a large real estate firm, was extremely sensitive about her weight and sought me out in private session. "I feel like a cow," she said, "and my husband is getting uncomfortable with our romantic life because of it. He doesn't say anything, but I can just tell. Since I was a child I was always told by my parents that I was just 'big-boned' and to get used to it." Linda was one of my most diligent clients and with the help of the Phoenix Solution, went on to lose about a third of her body weight. Not only did her love life improve, but she also developed the courage to seek out another more affirming executive position at a 25% increase in pay! The last I time I saw her she was slim, attractive, jubilant and successfully supervising a large office staff.

Larry Brooks attended a seminar I conducted. He was a factory worker, single parent, and had a cigarette habit that wouldn't quit. "I have smoked all my life, and have only been able to quit for about a half day at the most," he said, "so I don't think a little seminar is going to help." Despite his doubt, Larry paid close attention, learned the 5 steps of the Phoenix Solution and, by applying the steps, became a nonsmoker from that day forward. The same is true of my accountant, a 30 cigarettes a day smoker. I made him a deal: "I'll save your life, you save me money." He has become a nonsmoker, thanks to the Phoenix Solution, and my bill from him now smells like an envelope rather than an ashtray!

Bill Sebora, a well dressed insurance broker, came to me for help with his issues resulting from being a survivor of a dysfunctional family. After the first session he stopped drinking, and has not had a drop of alcohol for the past five years. He will tell you it is because of the Phoenix Solution that he is not only successful in business today, but in many areas of his personal life as well.

Many people have found that the powerful and versatile Phoenix Solution can be effectively utilized anywhere, anytime, and for any deliberate change one wishes to make in one's life. Why wait for circumstances to change you, when you can change circumstances?

The Unlimited Power of Psychotechnology

Throughout human history, the brightest and best minds have attempted to discover how people can live better and happier lives. Famous scientists like Leonardo da Vinci, Albert Einstein and David Bohm attempted to achieve intellectual happiness by understanding the physical laws that bind us. They succeeded in creating some of the most powerful changes in all of human history. Accomplished psychologists like Sigmund Freud, Abraham Maslow and Albert Ellis sought happiness through understanding the human mind and emotions, and their work has liberated many people from mental misery. Autogenics, the famous visualization technique developed by the Germans, has significantly boosted performance by athletes around the world for over two decades now.

Can you imagine the combined power of all of these fields finally harnessed and utilized by an individual? The new science of *Psychotechnology* builds upon the findings of the most accomplished and recognized scientists and philosophers in history. But knowledge alone is simply not enough. A way must be found to make it work for the individual.

The Latest Breakthrough: The Phoenix Solution

We are all seeking after the same basic goal in our every thought, word or action. The hard working laborer, the athlete, followers of religion, artists, chemical abusers, misers, executives, etc., are all striving–striving to overcome dissatisfaction and to *feel good*. One might say that all directed energy, whether deemed respectable or not, has some form of *feeling good* as its goal. Usually the source for our *feeling good* is sought "out there" somewhere. This drives us to worry and scheme in order to exert some control over those "out there" things and people in order to ensure a continuous supply of our *feeling good* prescriptions.

Many of the great seekers have missed the critical point (because they were also "out there" oriented) that what we really need is to be <u>our own supplier</u>. For most of our existence we were encouraged to put our lives in the care of others, and it never dawned on us that <u>we</u> could provide the requirements for feeling good to ourselves without assistance from any "out there" person, event, or thing. The purpose of this book is to help you rise from the ashes of this old-fashioned, inaccurate, and often destructive belief, and to place you in the pilot's seat of your life in ways you never dreamed possible, simply by utilizing the Phoenix Solution.

The Phoenix Solution is easy to use and the results will be surprisingly fast and effective. It not only works, but can be fun too. It is the most powerful way ever developed to put you in control of who you are now, and who you choose to become in the future.

CHAPTER 2

EVERY THOUGHT HAS POWER
The Freest People in The World
The Source of Power in You
To Be Truly Free
Four Truths You Can Believe In
The Seven Paralyzing Fears

Every single thought has power. Each thought you had in the past contributed to your being exactly what and where you are right now. Every thought you have from now on will determine what and where you will be in the near and distant future. Some thoughts are more powerful than others, and some are more powerful still. Thomas Alva Edison had the thought of running electricity across a wire in a glass globe, and lit up the world. Mr. Sears and Mr. Roebuck had the thought of selling clothes through a catalog, and became two of the world's most famous merchants. Cures for diseases, which saved many thousands of lives, started with but a single thought from historical figures such as Pasteur, Lister, Salk, and Sabine.

If a single thought can change our world, then certainly the right single thought can change your life for the better. Most of us grew up with a burning desire to be free to direct our own lives. So, why is it you are not? Do you frequently continue to experience life as being dictated by authority figures, your habits, money, your body, relationships, your emotions and the fear of death? Do you feel resentful of a promised something in life that continues to elude your grasp? Do you often settle for a suppressed sense of frustration and disappointment while filling in the days? Do you pretend to be in control, while inside you feel as if you live in a house of cards that could collapse at any moment? Today, perfectly normal people feel they have lost control of their lives. They feel dictated by the alarm clock that wakes them up, the commuting schedule, the boss, and the television habit, or the weekly shopping list. Perhaps you sense that there might be a way in which people can be in total control of their destiny and are obtaining from life everything they want. You are correct.

The Freest People In The World

There is a secret to escaping the dull grind that afflicts so many, and joining the happy few. The freest people in the world know how to think in a certain way. They know that by putting effort into certain patterns of thought they create magical outcomes in their lives. They know that the right form of thought puts them in the driver's seat of their lives, able to obtain all that they desire. You need not fall further and further behind in this life, left with only unfulfilled dreams, frustrated wishes and deep regrets.

THE FIRST TRUTH:
"Action brings about results, but all action is preceded by a particular thought. If we know the right thought, we get the desired results automatically."

The Source of Power in You

The power that propels your life comes from inside YOU. You may believe that power comes through you from some mystical source, but even then it must inevitably reside within you in order to be utilized. There is no reason for the Phoenix Solution to conflict with your personal spirituality, as it does not interfere with any interpretation of a higher power. Even if you firmly believe that God is geographically located "out there" somewhere, God must still manifest within you to be effective. This concept of power location is not unlike the fact that sunshine or nutrients must eventually be internalized by you if they are to benefit you. By all means, continue to hold the spiritual beliefs you currently hold, and utilize this manual in becoming even more effective in that faith. The Phoenix Solution is designed to empower anyone with the ability to think about thinking, and in that way is respectful of all faiths, or lack of faith.

THE SECOND TRUTH:
"You can fight ownership of and responsibility for your life as long as you wish, but eventually you will discover there simply is no other healthy choice."

<u>To Be Truly Free</u>

Some people believe that what you are about to learn is strange. Some believe that individuals do not have the ability to consciously determine their own lives. These beliefs are usually the result of childhood "tapes" that were programmed into us by authority figures. These "big people" ran our lives when we were little, and then it was smart for us to believe in everything they said and did. To be truly free in our lives today we must rise above those unnecessary, restrictive and outdated tapes. They no longer serve us well, and in fact, are like shackles that keep us from having everything we want in this life. We could spend a lot of time analyzing why those people believed in restriction. We could get into blaming them for our shortcomings today. We could even defend or justify why they did what they did. But do you really want to spend more of your precious life time on people who restricted you?

THE THIRD TRUTH:
"It is your right, your destiny, and your obligation to joyfully develop towards your ultimate knowledge and power."

You were given the abilities to develop yourself to your optimal potential (and just wait until you find out how *optimal* it really is!) and what a crime against yourself not to do that. What a crime of neglect against others to deny them the benefit of associating with your maximally developed powerful, wise, loving, sensitive, and strong human self!

The Seven Paralyzing Fears

Fear of physical pain is natural. Pay attention to warnings about physical danger, since they are life preservers: "Buckle Up!" "Watch for Falling Rocks!" "Caution, Dangerous Curve" and, "Look Both Ways!" It is also normal to have fear in other situations not involving danger of physical pain. This type of fear is called *anxiety*, and it is prevalent in our lives today. Anxiety arises in us for one of two reasons: 1) We are reluctant to move outside our *comfort zone*; or, 2) We feel unprepared to deal with the unexpected. The end result of anxiety is that we become paralyzed by the mere anticipation of any of the following:

The fear of making a mistake
The fear of being criticized
The fear of losing someone's affection
The fear of appearing foolish or insane
The fear of upsetting habits or traditions
The fear of being excluded or ostracized
The fear of realizing our true identity

The first six fears boil down to a negative outlook based on the thought, "I don't want to be wrong." It doesn't take rocket scientist thinking to deduce why you grew up with such an aversion to being wrong, BUT just in case you need a little reminder, here they are from A-Z:

When you were "wrong" you may have been
   a) physically punished
   b) called "silly" or "stupid"
   c) made fun of
   d) frowned at

e) denied privileges or food
f) shunned
g) denied affection
h) shamed
i) guilted
j) laughed at
k) intimidated
l) given a low grade
m) molested
n) criticized
o) yelled at
p) made to feel insane
q) humiliated
r) sent away
s) threatened with horrible consequences (I'll skin you alive/I wish you were dead/Wait'll your father comes home/You'll roast in hell/ etc.)
t) told you were evil/bad/sinful/a devil or demon
u) told you would be the death of your parent
v) isolated in a room/closet/basement/car
w) threatened with an object (belt/stick/switch club/hand/paddle/knife/gun/etc.)
x) given an increased workload
y) grounded
z) threatened with a loss of credibility and/or status

Do any of these affect you while reading them? Well, of course, they do. We carry these with us into adulthood and they resonate in our very tissues when we anticipate making a mistake. <u>They also resonate when we anticipate trying something new</u>, and this can keep us from developing our full potential. What a crime against ourselves to let these old tapes limit us today. When you wish to grow and cannot, it creates frustration and resentment–a toxic internal environment. To counteract this: When those old limiting tapes start increasing in volume as you anticipate trying something new, replace them with this one: **"I am attempting to *learn* right now!"**

"A man learns to ice skate by staggering around making a fool of himself...indeed, we progress in all things by resolutely making fools of ourselves."

—George Bernard Shaw

The Seventh Fear

The fear of realizing our true identity is a bit complex. We are basically not who we usually think we are. Within the human is incredible power, incredible intelligence, and incredible passion, including the passion of all the emotions...especially joy. But how often do you fully experience your "true self"? How often do you feel super powerful, super intelligent, and super joyous? My experience is that people are so conditioned to feeling full of worry, doubt, and powerlessness, that they have come to see these false states as reality! They buy the delusion to the extent that they have developed an actual fear of their true identity. Perhaps Sigmund Freud said it best:

"The cause of most psychological illness is the fear of knowledge of oneself---of one's emotions, impulses, memories, capacities, potentialities, and of one's destiny."

Is it possible that all along we have been capable of making all of our dreams come true, but didn't know it? How could this happen? Again, one way it happened was that we were "seduced" into believing that our source of power was "out there," when indeed it was not. We have continued to look for happiness and satisfaction by grasping at "out there" things, only to find them temporarily satisfying at best.

THE FOURTH TRUTH:
"If what you want is not what you need you will never get enough."

We grasped at apparitions, and grasped for more when those did not satisfy us. Perhaps we were looking in the wrong direction. Grasping for and receiving another paycheck, another compliment, another tidbit of food, another knickknack, another relationship, has never held us for long, has it? There has been that nagging feeling that something was missing, or that things were just a little too precarious, or superfluous, or hollow.

Perhaps you have felt that you didn't know who you were...and at the same time you were afraid of knowing your real self. That is the 7th fear. You are more powerful than you ever realized, and the fear you may have experienced in becoming your true self is usually a mixture of confusion and awe from that potential power. You are entitled to immense power because your destiny is not to wait on handouts, or run from one tidbit to the next, or to constantly worry whether or not life will take care of you. You have a much grander purpose. The Phoenix Solution will give you bountiful tools to deal with any fear you might have as you move along the path of empowerment. Keep your chin up, keep reading and working through this book, and remember:

**Courage is not fearlessness---
Courage is going on despite the fear.**

You already have courage. You have demonstrated it many times in your life. Remember?

CHAPTER 3

THE PSYCHOTECHNOLOGICAL SOLUTION
The History of Psychotechnology
The Nine Principles

What is this marvelous new science? Psychotechnology is the most powerful new psychology for improving your life that has ever existed. To better understand, let's look at the word *psychotechnology* itself. It represents a dynamic and powerful blend of two fields of endeavor.

> PSYCHOLOGY: The science of the mind or of mental states and processes.
> TECHNOLOGY: The application of knowledge for practical ends.

Therefore:

> PSYCHOTECHNOLOGY: A body of knowledge, including theories and techniques, dedicated to understanding and influencing individual, group and societal behavior in specified situations by deliberate alteration of mental processes.

Or, to state it more clearly for an individual's application:

> *Psychotechnology is the science of individual ability to deliberately alter moods, behaviors, and even life patterns with the optimal application of a primary thought.*

Or, to boil it down even further:

> **Psychotechnology is the science of individual empowerment —the power to create one's life in any manner one chooses.**

The History of Psychotechnology

It is helpful to place Psychotechnology in an historical perspective. For generations many thinkers, writers, psychologists, and religious leaders espoused a reality of "no hope from within." If there was a glimmer of salvation it was through luck, providence, or some outside being taking mercy on us. Historically we call these the "doomsayers." The next wave of thinkers spoke more optimistically and talked about having hope, but with no evidence. They, in effect were wishing mightily, but without evidence or ability. Some of these were false prophets, some desperate people, and some were just Pollyannas. Then came a wave of pioneers who actually brought us to the shore of the river of empowering knowledge and said, "You see that island over there? There is such a thing as freedom from life's misery. We can't get you there, but at least we have proven it exists!" These were the visionaries. Next came a wave of psychological architects who built the bridges and boats to reach the island and said, "Here we are—able to truly repair ourselves!" These were the healers. Then came another group who said, "Look! Further beyond the island is another shoreline! We are just in midstream here on the island. Over there is the actualization of our full potential, not just healing our illnesses—but the possibility of rising above the ashes of ordinary existence." These were another wave of visionaries called "new agers." And then there are those of us who are putting the new bridge together, the one that will reach the next island. We are the psychotechnologists...the psychonauts...the explorers of the inner jungle...the transformers. We are the ultimate product and process of humanity seeking its essence—people creating permanent shifts in their lives deliberately! It is the most incredible adventure ever embarked upon. It makes Christopher Columbus look like a boy scout on a weekend camporee.

How long have people attempted to change their lives by changing their minds? You can bet cave people spun around and got dizzy just for the thrill of it. It's a picture. Somewhere up the line people probably started chanting because it was temporarily pleasing, and eventually they began to pray for help to provide temporary feelings of security. Eventually all the various yogas showed up with physical posturings, verbalizations, and deliberate thought altering designed to still the mind, contact a god, purify the self, etc. Impatient people with the same goal of changing things became scientists in an attempt to speed things up through organization, controllability, and predictability. Scientists were usually not very creative people, but generally they provided some productive insights into how things do and don't work. It is important to remember that although the real reason for these endeavors was so that people could feel better "in here" they were still emphasizing "out there" sources of power.

As a psychotherapist and consultant, I found that many people wanted to change their lives for the better permanently. "I have tried everything," said Mr. Hartman. "Exercise, self-talk, meditation; they all seemed to work for about a month or less. Nothing ever made a permanent difference in my life."

Mr. Hartman is a professional, but I have heard the same complaint from so many people. There are many ideas and programs, but none that seem to make a permanent difference. Is something being overlooked, I wondered? It had to be possible for people to have the individual ability to permanently change their lives for the better without depending continually on sources of power outside themselves. It was from this thought that I created the field of Psychotechnology from the term *psychotechnology*. How appropriate that the conception of the field came from but a single thought! But when you think about it, each of us probably started with a single thought. Whether it was a "glint in your daddy's eye" or your parents making a conscious decision to have a child, look what has happened as a result of that single thought!

This angle of vision is the same angle necessary to look at the potential for bringing about change in our lives. With but a single thought we can move mountains, if you happen to be in a mountain-moving mood! The thought does not move the mountain. The first thought sets other thoughts in motion much like the primary domino in a chain reaction of dominoes. <u>The specifications of the first thought are critical if the thought is to have power.</u> This is the foundation of Psychotechnology—the science of the empowered primary thought that can create magic in your life.

In the early 1980's I became aware of the pain inherent in survivors of low functioning families. These individuals grew up still bearing the internal pain and handicaps typical of any abused and neglected living being. Some developed into criminals and/or alcohol and other chemical addicts, but all suffered in intimate relationships with others and, most importantly, in that all-important intimate relationship with self. Although some pretended otherwise, all suffered inside from doubt, anxiety, and a deeply felt sense of hurt. In my counseling work, I began to see just how slow traditional therapy was for these suffering people. Their wounds were too deep for a once-a-week talk session to do much good.

It was during this time that I began seeking ways to speed up the painful work of recovery for these people. The key word for me was *acceleration*. I researched ways to accelerate healing, growth and change in people's lives. I was on fire. I attended many seminars, workshops, conferences, trainings, and constantly used myself as a guinea pig to see what worked, how it worked, and how it could work better. I began to combine the best pieces of each until it became clear to me, that what was called for was a new field—a field dedicated to the study of individual empowerment. Since establishing the field of *Psychotechnology*, I have become aware of many marketers of various self-improvement techniques. I have seen the selling of tapes, gadgets, books, goggles, and substances that promise self-improvement. Some of these work for short periods, and some don't work at all. The major drawback is that most all of them are still "out there" oriented, and do not truly empower the individual to uncover their raw talents and maximize their potential in an ongoing, unassisted manner. It was then that I decided there had to be standards or principles in the field of Psychotechnology if it was to have credibility and validity.

The Principles of Psychotechnology

Principles are the form, the glue, and the guidance system of any field of endeavor. They are statements about beliefs and values held by those interested in that particular area of study. It is important to know exactly what a field's principles are before one invests energy in that field. Principles should be openly stated, and subject to examination, question, debate and the possibility of alteration based upon new knowledge. There are nine simple principles that underlie the new science of Psychotechnology.

THE NINE PRINCIPLES OF PSYCHOTECHNOLOGY

1. People have the ability to think and do.

2. People have the ability to grow and develop.

3. People can change outcomes through decision-making.

4. All human change begins with a primary thought.

5. People can decide at any moment to switch from being directed by others and circumstances to being self-directed.

6. Human experience is human reality, and is subjectively interpreted and validated.

7. People can modify the impact of their personal history upon themselves.

8. Human effort is best served by elegant honesty and integrity.

9. Humans are spiritual beings, and are more than the apparent sum of their parts.

<u>The First Principle</u>: **People have the ability to think and do.**

Everyone has within themselves the ability to think of something and then do it. The thought precedes the action. Have you ever turned on the television or bought something without first having the thought to do it? Thoughts are so natural that we may not be aware of them. By the time we reach adulthood, many of our actions are instinctive and seemingly without thought.

We are not always consciously aware of our thoughts, but aware or not, each thought is registered in the chemistry and electricity of our brains. The registered thought can then act to produce a result. This is how the human brain and body work today, and how they always have.

Not much has changed about how the mind and body function, but how we utilize those functions certainly has changed. At one time scientists such as James Watson and B. F. Skinner believed we were merely a series of habituated reflex actions, much like the automatic behavior that happens to your leg when the doctor hits your knee with that nasty little hammer. Today we know that we have capabilities other than just responding. We have the ability to think about what we are going to do before we do it. Of more importance, we have learned that we can think about our thoughts, and even <u>choose</u> the type of thinking we will do. The lingo for this is *metacognition*, being consciously aware about our thinking. This ability is what makes the human being so remarkable—and powerful!

The Second Principle: **People have the ability to grow and develop.**

Once you were an infant. Then it was time to go to kindergarten. There were other schools after that, but even after you left school, you were still learning, developing and growing. Many of us are very surprised just how much we learned in our 20's. We were surprised because schools, friends and elders kept talking about "when you grow up" like it was a final stage. The implication was that once you reached 18 or 21 or graduated from college, etc., you would be "done" with all that growing and stretching stuff. What a surprise to find out that graduation was a beginning more than it was an ending!

Today there are many courses in colleges on adult development, and in those courses it is common knowledge that adults have stages of development just as children do. Students of human development discover that a person never stops developing unless they choose to stop; that our potential as human beings is endless.

It is the natural order of things for us to constantly be learning and stretching our capabilities. *Could it be that so many people are unhappy today because they have forgotten how to grow, or have locked themselves into places in their lives where they feel they are unable to develop?* It makes us unhappy to be restrained from our destiny, and from the wonderful vitality of the growing processes that it takes to get us there!

The Third Principle: **People can change outcomes through decision-making.**

People make decisions and change outcomes all the time. Shall I go to the movie? Yes. And the outcome of my evening is different than if I had said "No." Shall I get drunk until I am sick? No, I will only have two beers. And the outcome is different. Shall I buy this dress or put the money in savings? Whichever I decide, the outcome will be decided as well.

All day long we face one fork in the road after another. Whichever fork we decide to choose will determine the outcomes in our lives. It is easy, although painful sometimes, to see this retrospectively in our past. Almost as if viewing a roadmap, we can look back and see where we made major differences in our lives just by one simple decision after another. I know a fellow who mailed inquiries to every branch of the service on the same day and decided that he would join the one who replied first. It was the Marines. His life has been different to this day because of that one whimsical decision. Who you decided to associate with, how you spent your money, where you decided to live, all brought you to where you are today—the consequences of your decisions. This same pattern will continue in your future.

The Fourth Principle: **All human change begins with a primary thought.**

Have you ever attempted to determine how you arrived at a certain topic in a conversation? Did you begin to backtrack to find the source of the thinking---to find the "seed" thought that started it all? Remember the feeling when you found it? It was funny, wasn't it? You marveled at how all those ideas and conversation and emotions flowed from just one thought.

Several years ago a fellow made a lot of guest appearances at malls and on television. He would set up huge displays of dominoes, some that covered an area as large as a gymnasium floor. The dominoes spelled out words, or made pictures or portraits. Some dominoes were colored to create beautiful patterns, some climbed miniature staircases, and some swung like Tarzan on little ropes when they were struck. Days were spent setting up the elaborate demonstration. As the time drew near, so did the crowds and cameras. The anticipation was exhilarating. A hush would fall over the crowd before the fellow would finally step forward and, with a flourish, initiate the whole display by starting a primary domino falling in a certain direction. What followed was extraordinary. People laughed, cheered and applauded at the beauty and intricacy of....what? Connections. Connections that created marvelous patterns...all beginning with a PRIMARY DOMINO.

Our thought patterns each begin with a single thought, and they create a marvelous display, known as *your life*. Each single thought we have can spin off into many areas of thought with the behaviors that may follow. Thoughts can also just dead-end and go nowhere, or even be circular, like a dog chasing it's tail, and go nowhere in a hurry. But know these fundamental truths about thought:

1) Every single thought has some power.

2) Each one you had in the past contributed to your being exactly what and where you are right now. (No, it wasn't fate, luck, or coincidence.)

3) Every single thought you have from now on will determine what and where you will be in the near and distant future.

4) Some thoughts are more powerful than others...and some are more powerful still.

It becomes obvious that it can be of tremendous benefit to pay attention to our thoughts, especially those we endow with Primary Domino power.

<u>The Fifth Principle</u>: **People can decide at any moment to switch from being directed by others and circumstances to being self-directed.**

We were born small <u>and</u> dependent. Everybody around us was bigger, stronger and more experienced. We let others direct our lives a great deal. Eventually we learned to direct our own lives some of the time. Today we can decide when we want to let others (or circumstances) direct us, or when we want to decide for ourselves.

<u>The Sixth Principle</u>: **Human experience is human reality, and is subjectively interpreted and validated.**

For centuries humans have contemplated the question, "What *is* "reality"? People have come up with many, many theoretical answers. This is not a difficult issue! Let's just talk about what we *know*. We *know* we have experiences. We *know* experiences are real to *us*. We *know* that people don't always see things the same way. We know the way people see things is the way they experience them; that is <u>their</u> "reality." This is why we argue. When we argue we are trying to make someone see an experience *our* way. What we are saying in an argument is, "My reality is better than yours." This is actually rarely the case. Everyone's reality seems well-suited to them if you step back and take an objective look at each individual's life. But who has the time, inclination, or expertise to perform a case study on each person with whom you disagree? It is easier and more elegant for you to accept the following as a motto: *"Just because you and I disagree doesn't mean one of us is wrong."*

And this even deeper transformational
TRUTH:
Circumstances do not create a person, they reflect a person.

This is a rather shattering statement, is it not? If you will make just this truth part of your life, things will begin to change for you. It is a Primary Domino of understanding and freedom.

<u>The Seventh Principle</u>: **People can modify the impact of their personal history upon themselves.**

You have done this many times. We have all received new information or a new angle of vision regarding a past event that has changed the impact of the original event upon us. Frank Slusser came to me angry about his dysfunctional family upbringing. He felt he had been neglected and abandoned. He had to grow up basically on his own. I helped him feel his anger, which he certainly had a right to have; every child deserves a loving, nurturing home. But one day Frank realized it was the desertion in his childhood that had helped him develop the skills needed to start, run and prosper in his own business. It was his resentment about his childhood that was raining on his parade, not his actual past experiences. With that realization he permanently shifted his feelings from unfinished anger to gratitude for the gifts those circumstances gave him. His history was changed—and after all those years!

Shorter versions of this happen to us all the time. Sunny Cowen was going to a prayer meeting with three of her friends when her car stalled and drifted to the side of the highway. Angry at her old car, and upset that she couldn't get it to start, she and her friends decided to wait for the highway patrol. After 20 minutes and no police, she decided to try starting the car again, and it did! Proceeding around the next curve on the highway she found her highway patrolman. He was busy stopping traffic because of a huge accident which involved many cars and caused many serious injuries, which had occurred 30 minutes before! In relating the story to me years later Sunny said, "I could have kissed that old car on the nose!"

Often we look back on events in our lives and realize they were for the best, although we ranted and raved at the time. Wouldn't you like the ability to know events are for the best as they occur, instead of waiting for it to *maybe* dawn on you *someday*? Imagine the feeling of knowing instant gratitude for whatever happens in your life! Imagine internalizing this truth:

"No matter what happens to me, I am going to benefit from it one way or another."

With that mindset, you always win no matter what happens, and without giving up your privilege of protesting wrongdoing either!

The Eighth Principle: **Human effort is best served by elegant honesty and integrity.**

Psychotechnology is about truth, the liberating type of truth. And it is about power, the liberating type of power. It is about freeing people to self-design their own lives in the way they see fit. It is a vehicle to get you to where you want to be. Automobiles do that in a way. Some people use them responsibly to get from one place to another more efficiently. Some misuse automobiles and create harm for themselves and others. Although people do gain things through dishonesty, it is only because they have never felt the power of the deeper truths of the human being. In reality they have settled for less; what they achieved through dishonest means is a drop in the bucket compared to what they could have had by applying those same energies honestly.

It is important to use elegant (as opposed to "brutal") honesty and honorable intentions in applications of your newly acquired power. You may make errors in judgement with the Phoenix Solution, but honest mistakes will benefit you. On the other hand, misusing power towards unscrupulous ends is not a psycho-technological prerogative. It is important to respect yourself and others as well as the process. There is no need not to, since you can have anything you want faster and better the honest and elegant way.

<u>The Ninth Principle</u>: **Humans are spiritual beings, and are more than the apparent sum of their parts.**

You are not just a bunch of tissue that happens to think. You are more than an accumulation of reflexes that happens to move. People have much higher orders of possible existence open to them. Some have experienced it and <u>know</u> this to be true. Others surmise or hope it is true. *It is true.* Many have risen above their history, their circumstances, and their ailments to prosper in this lifetime. They did it through tapping into that part of themselves that is difficult to describe, but is, nonetheless, real: That invisible part of you that gives meaning, sustenance and vitality to life.

CHAPTER 4

TAKE CHARGE OF YOUR LIFE
Your Locus of Control
Limits & Boundaries
Power
Two Truths You Can Believe In
Six Excuses For Staying Powerless

If you are not aware that you are in control of your life, it is understandable. Your first experiences with control were when you were born. And since you were born small and dependent, you had very little ability to control anything. Everyone in your universe was bigger, more experienced, and seemed to know more than you did about everything. Sometimes they convinced you of this with love. Sometimes they convinced you of this with fear. They even convinced you that <u>they</u> knew what <u>you</u> needed. "Eat this; it's good for you." "Do this, or you will be sorry." "Do that, or you'll get sick." No wonder we grew up with a tendency to trust other people's judgements more than our own! As adults it can still be confusing and difficult to know when we should listen to others and when we should be our own boss.

TRUTH:
Part A
"You are the resident expert on what your needs are."
Part B
"You have the right to determine how your needs will be met."

Being told what your needs are teaches you not to develop a trust in your own internal sense of what is best and true for you. When this is done to you, it has very powerful effects. The erroneous thought that you don't know what is best for yourself was probably placed in your consciousness long before you knew you had a choice about it. At the time it was wise to go along with the program since the authority figures implanting this erroneous thought were also the keepers of the food and the affection. Often the needs they convinced us were our own, were actually their needs. Believing that we didn't know what was best for us was our first sellout on ourselves. Since then we have been told so many times what to do, how to do it, how not to do it and what we needed, that we have forgotten a very important truth: Nobody is supposed to know what we need better than we do.

Our choices today consist mostly of going along with what we were convinced of in our early years. The major thought that controlled us then and still can today is: *"If you don't _____ then bad things will happen."* If you don't do what Dad says he will punish you. If you don't do what Mom says, you will get a frown. If you don't do what teacher says, you will get an F. If you don't eat your meat, you can't have any pudding. If you don't do what the supervisor wants, you won't get a raise. If you continue in this fashion, I will abandon you.

Unfortunately, no one ever served notice to our subconscious mind that childhood was over. No one officially declared that we could stop being threatened and seduced into buying this erroneous notion that we don't know what is best for us. So let's make it official:

You, and only you, are supposed to be in charge of your life. Only you can truly know your needs and act or not act on them. Life cannot be lived for you. You get to live it now.

This will make life much easier and much, much more fun, and healthier too! You will no longer feel manipulated by others, or as if you are living life from a "have to" posture, i.e. no more resentments towards anyone or anything (except yourself when you refuse to use your new tools and skills!). The Phoenix Solution is a form of psychotechnology designed to help you get comfortable with and efficient in running your own life. Think of this manual as a friendly hand on your rear fender after the training wheels have been removed! At first it may be uncomfortable. The power you will possess may seem dizzying. The responsibility may appear overwhelming. The uncertainty resident in any new endeavor can be anxiety-producing, like riding the bike without the training wheels for the first time. Remember: It is supposed to feel uncomfortable, anxiety-producing, or even dizzying at first. This is the natural response system to change. **This is just temporary.**

Your Locus of Control

Locus comes from the Latin word for **place**. In a human, *locus of control* denotes where the source of one's power is felt to be located. If you have an **internal** locus of control you see a high correlation between your choices and the outcomes in your life. If you have an **external** locus of control, you see little correlation between your choices and the outcomes in your life.

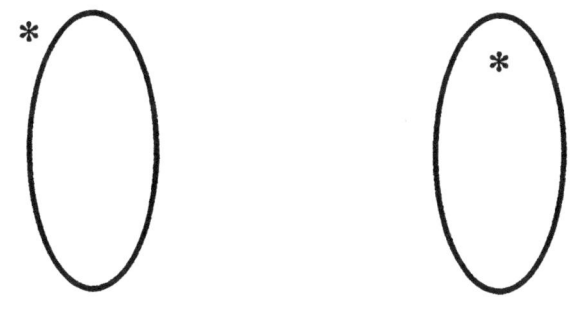

External Locus of Control   Internal Locus of Control
Empowerment ======>

Victim; irresponsible;   Empowered; responsible;
Unhealthy and dependent;   Healthy;
Little ability to do anything   Ability to make good
but suffer/hope or enjoy   things occur and fully
handouts.   enjoy the results

Empowerment is the process of moving from an external locus of control to an internal locus of control. It denotes actualization of the potentiality of the person to self-design his/her world.

Limits and Boundaries

Make it one of your goals to realize you have an *internal locus of control*, because the truth is, you really do! You establish your locus of control best by deliberately choosing to set healthy limits and boundaries. *Limits* are how far you will let yourself go. *Boundaries* are how far you will let other people go.

Examples of *limits*:

"I am going to walk two miles today."
"I will do the dishes later."
"I will refrain from using profanity."
"I will not call Bill today."
"I am going to eat 2200 calories today."
"I will rest and relax all day Sunday."
"I will obey the Scout Law."

Examples of *boundaries*:

"You can't talk to me that way."
"No, you cannot borrow $5, because you never repay me when you say you will."
"You can touch me, but you can't touch me like that."
"You kids will have to fix your own lunch today."
"I won't tolerate degrading sexual innuendos from you."
"Please don't call me anymore."
"Please don't let your dog come into my yard."

Power
==========

Power is an odd thing. If you believe you have it, you do, and if you believe you don't, you don't! Most people wish they had more power. But almost everyone fails to realize the truth about the source of that power, which makes the power impossible to find!

TRUTH:
"All of your power comes from within."

You do not have to go anywhere, or to anyone, or buy anything, to have more power—you already have it! Your issue with power is not finding it, but in effectively using what you already have. In other words, it is a delusion (an untruth that is believed to be true) that you are powerless. Humans with an external locus of control are living a delusional existence...no wonder they feel so anxious!
This truth does make the job of empowerment a lot easier than if you had to locate power somewhere "out there." You must, however, be willing to uncover the power you do have. Why wouldn't you be willing to uncover the power you possess? So glad you asked.

Six Excuses for Staying Powerless
----

1) If I don't have power, I don't have to be responsible.
2) If I don't have power, it's not my fault when things don't work out.
3) It takes too much effort/initiative to use power.
4) People expect a lot from you when you have power.
5) If you have power, some people won't like you or will try to take it away.
6) "Good" people/Christians/citizens/followers/etc. shouldn't have too much power.

And, of course, these are all true for you if you believe them to be true. They are not The Truth. They are just true for you because you believe them to be so. It is much more to your advantage to believe in objective truth about power. You will benefit healthfully along with everyone who comes in contact with you. The powerless route is one filled with ignorance, poor health, frustration, negativity, fear and other unfun things. Let us promptly refute the excuses for staying powerless.

1) If I don't have power, I don't have to be responsible.

You have been responsible for how you interact with life since you were conceived (and maybe even before!). No one can get into your skin and decide how to deal or not deal with life, because that skin is already occupied by **you**. All your wishes and arguments to the contrary won't change this simple truth. The only real choice has been whether or not to accept this fact of life.

I met Janet in a laundromat on a Sunday afternoon. She was a worn out looking 50 year-old woman folding a big stack of men's jeans. "Great way to spend a sunny afternoon, isn't it?" I quipped. She sighed, "Yes, if I could get these boys to live on their own I wouldn't have to be here." "How old are your boys?" I asked. "23 and 27," Janet replied, "They both work construction, and still live at home." "Why don't you ask them to live on their own?" I, perhaps impertinently, replied. She sighed again, "Boy, that would be nice, but how can I do that?" "Well, you could start by slipping a note into those jeans saying, 'Enjoy these clean jeans, guys, because they are the last ones I'm doing.' Then you could do the same with the lunch box I suspect you prepare for them everyday: 'Enjoy this lunch, boys, because it's the last one I'm preparing.' If they don't get the hint, then put a note on their pillow saying, 'Enjoy this bed tonight...' " Janet sighed again (something I suspect she did a lot), "That would be so nice, but how do I do that?" Janet could not see that she was choosing to remain powerless so she wouldn't have to be responsible for throwing out her grownup, but still dependent, men-kids. Notice how this shirking of responsibility doesn't change the <u>amount</u> of work you still have to do? In Janet's case it appeared she was actually working harder at something she didn't want to do by refusing the apparent "burden" of responsibility. How ironic and how sad.

2) If I don't have power, it's not my fault when things don't work out.

Sure it is. If you gave up your responsibility (power), you share the blame <u>whether you admit it or not</u>. If you didn't actually cause woundings or problems, you still share in the responsibility for the healing and solving. And, by the way, why worry so much about "fault"? If it actually <u>was</u> your fault when something went wrong, it's O.K., you aren't supposed to be perfect...or hadn't you noticed?

Teresa said in session one day, "My son Derek is so unhappy. His father insists on his going to law school, and Derek wants to be a teacher. I just hate to see him hurting like this. I think he should be allowed to follow his dream of teaching." "Why can't he?" I asked. "Because his father pays the tuition, and that's what he wants." "Have you spoken up on this?" I asked. "I can't really, Harry earns the money and he is paying Derek's tuition. I just hope he's happy when Derek is miserable, or even flunks out." "But Teresa, aren't you going to hurt if Derek hurts?" "Yes, I'm his Mother, of course I will hurt. But it won't be my fault." Teresa won't speak her mind just so she doesn't have to assume responsibility, even though she knows people, including herself, are going to be in pain. Chances are the pain she is saving by shirking her responsibility will not even come close to the pain she will experience for a long time to come, not to mention Derek's pain. It <u>is</u> Teresa's fault that she did not assume the responsibility she should have assumed in these circumstances.

3) It takes too much effort/initiative to use power.

You are actually expending the same amount of effort no matter what you are doing...watching television or working in the garden or writing a letter or jogging. Life energy is not measured in calorie expenditure, but is a very personal investment we call "time." In other words, it takes just as much "time" to watch an hour of television as it does to work in the garden for an hour, etc. What is really operating in this excuse for staying powerless is the uneasiness caused by moving outside your *comfort zone*. Effort is not the issue at all. In reality, it takes extra energy to suppress effort, since our molecules are in constant motion and are naturally inclined to do things all the time.

I see in people the effects of not maintaining their health through proper physical exercise. Their response is that it just takes too much energy and time. "I am already tired," they say, "I wouldn't have any energy at all if I worked out!" I'm going to ask you, the reader, to refute this for yourself. Ask five people who work out regularly if they have more or less energy because they exercise. I guarantee that they will say, to a person, that they have more energy because they exercise. And while you have them buttonholed, ask them this question: "How do you find the time to exercise?" They will tell you explicitly. Time and energy are actually elastic. It is your mind that is not. The Phoenix Solution will fix that!

4) People expect a lot from you when you have power.

Like they don't when you don't! People expect a lot from people on welfare and people like Donald Trump. Expectations from others is a constant. This is a worrisome carryover from childhood when people were always holding up a high bar and expecting you to jump over it. "You can do better than that!" "Why aren't you as good as Terry/Mike/Lin/Dancing Waters?" Expectations are usually critical in nature.

Expectations are like handcuffs; they measure you against outcomes. And, of course, you always come up short. It's the nature of the beast. No one speaks of expectations if something has already been accomplished! Expectations are only mentioned when there is a perceived shortfall. We must be aware of expectations of others, the world, and especially of ourselves, that we do not create and sustain a prison of our own making.

Goals, however, are different <u>and</u> very important. They give direction, meaning and a sense of accomplishment. The deadening question is, "What do they expect of me?" The liberating question is, "What is my mission, and what can help me accomplish it?" It is very intelligent to consider your mission whenever you are about to invest your resources (time, $, energy, self) in order to align yourself in the most healthfully powerful manner.

5) If you have power, some people won't like you or will try to take it away.

People are hungry for and scared of power at the same time; i.e., it is <u>very</u> attractive. People want power so they can solve all their problems and get what they want. People are afraid of it because they have seen what Hitler-types, military leaders, politicians, criminals, and angry parents have done with it. People are also afraid of the "feeling" of power because it is a very heady experience, and they are simply unused to it. Trust this: It's a feeling you can get used to! You <u>will</u> need to learn to wisely use your power with those drawn to you.

6) "Good" people/Christians/citizens/followers/etc., shouldn't have power.

This is a ruse perpetuated by powerless people who don't know how to be otherwise. If there is one thing every great leader (including religious ones) possessed, it was power. How can you truly do "good deeds" without power? With no power you can just barely benefit yourself and will, of necessity, be totally occupied with doing just that. You will also drain those you are forced to rely upon. This planet of ours is facing some major crises. It needs powerful people to help preserve resources, not powerless people to drain them.

I remember a client being in constant emotional pain due to her marriage to an addictive spouse. Her usual statement to herself was a big sigh followed by, "If it's God's will, he will straighten up someday." In other words, she was saying: "It's not up to me to do anything about my life. Let God do it." I reminded her that God had given her a brain and willpower to utilize in solving these things herself.

Some people try to have power over others by remaining helpless. These people don't know any other way to get their needs met. Their self-sufficiency tools and skills are dormant. But, no one wants to feel like a leech. The Phoenix Solution is the total opposite of "leechdom."

To summarize: You are accountable for your power. If you misuse your power, you are accountable. If you remain powerless, you are accountable for that as well.

CHAPTER 5

THE COMFORT ZONE
What runs your life
Two ways to eliminate friction

Have you ever wondered what keeps you from changing? What prevents you from just dropping certain thoughts, words or behaviors in the wink of an eye, and then picking up brand new ones? Think about the delight in having the kind of personal power that would enable you to choose to be a non-smoker, or detach from a destructive relationship, or instantly change your mood from one of anxiety to one of euphoria. Imagine making any of those things happen simply and quickly! Why can't we? What keeps us stuck in old patterns we either don't or shouldn't want any more?

Your comfort zone runs your life. Think about the implications of this statement! Your comfort zone is your personal space of behaviors (thoughts/words/actions) in which you feel comfortable. Needless to say, many of the behaviors with which you are "comfy" are not beneficial for you in the long run! It's comfortable to continue eating potato chips (which can be 50% oil). It's comfortable to continue smoking cigarettes (cancer sticks). It's comfortable to not get exercise when you need it (the couch potato syndrome).

Usually when we think of comfort, external things come to mind such as clothes, furniture, temperature, companions. But much more pertinent to the purposes of the Phoenix Solution is the comfort zone each person carries *inside* them. Without an understanding of the internal comfort zone, personal growth and change will happen only against the greatest of resistance, if at all.

Comfort zones and the accompanying warning signs they provide are different for every person. They are mostly a product of our cultural and familial upbringing. We all have learned emotional signals that warn us "You are now leaving your comfort zone!" sounding very much as if a Klingon vessel has uncloaked in our front yard. Think how invested we are in our own zone. Realize that others are just as invested in theirs. Discrepancies in comfort zones are undoubtedly the source of most arguments. When people disagree, it is mostly their respective comfort zones arguing with each other. We can eliminate future friction instantly with a new thinking on this:

"I may not agree with what you say, but I will defend to the death your right to say it."

This is the principle on which the United States was founded. We gave each other the fundamental right to have our own comfort zone of beliefs, words, and actions, as long as it brought no harm to others.

Guess what? We can even be more enlightened than this in our relations with others! We can allow ourselves to know that <u>of course</u> everyone's comfort zone is different. Because we each have different backgrounds, learned responses, ways of interpreting reality, etc., we are naturally going to possess comfort zones that are different from one another. It would actually be very odd if we all felt the same way about everything. Know this: <u>We are only bothered by differences in others because we perceive those differences as threatening us to move outside our own comfort zone.</u> So, we seemingly have no choice but to make them wrong in order to validate the strong investment we have in our own comfort zone. Get it? Let's again remember:

"Just because we don't agree doesn't mean one of us is wrong."

Stop being threatened by others' comfort zones—they've worked just as hard to build theirs as you have worked to build yours. It's not your place to threaten theirs any more than you want your own threatened. You probably have enough to do maintaining <u>or</u> changing your own. If you have made the mistake of building specific people and/or specific people's specific behaviors into your comfort zone permanently, then you must look at that. Making other people part of the thermostatic controls for your comfort zone is a grievous setup for anxiety, friction and resentment. The syndrome of *co-dependence* that has risen to social awareness recently is indicative of this very serious issue. (Most mall bookstores also have plenty of paperbacks on the subject, and I strongly urge you to avail yourself of lots of reading on this topic if it is pertinent to you.) At the root of co-dependence is an internal inability to set healthy limits and boundaries. Just remember that one of the rights you do not have in a democratic society is to utilize another human being as an indispensable gear in the machinery of your comfort zone!

A final and very important note on comfort zone: In order to make effective transitions in your life, there must be a willingness to challenge your personal comfort zone. Learn to be comfortable with the idea that one must temporarily experience discomfort in order to transform experience and, consequently, replace the old restrictive comfort zone with a new and more rewarding one. The Phoenix Solution will make this much easier for you to do.

CHAPTER 6

THE PHOENIX SOLUTION
Introduction
The Unity of Experience
The Essential Five Steps of The Phoenix Solution

<u>Introduction</u>

The Phoenix Solution is the most powerful tool for self actualization ever discovered. It is so powerful, that I have seen it succeed even for people who have never enjoyed success before. The Phoenix Solution is one form of psychotechnology and is simple to understand, easy to use, and costs no more than the price of this book. With psychotechnology you do not need any electronics, crystals, tapes, music, special surroundings or other people in order to succeed. It is the ultimate independent process. One merely needs knowledge of the Phoenix Solution and a conscious mind for it to work. Sound like magic? It *is*...the natural magic you were born with taken to the ultimate realization of your potential. The process of using the Phoenix Solution moves you in the direction of supreme self-reliance. It uncovers potential powers you never knew existed inside you. It maximizes those powers like a ruby crystal does when transforming an ordinary ray of light into a powerful laser beam. The Phoenix Solution can be quietly utilized anytime, anywhere, enhancing not only you, but everything and everyone around you!

<u>The Unity of Experience</u>

We may disagree on a lot of things, but the one thing we can agree on is that we have *experience*, or conscious awareness of our involvement in life. No matter where you locate your experience, it always happens inside you, in your consciousness. Try to imagine having an experience without being conscious of it! This is a very convenient truth for our purposes. If all experience happens inside you, and you are the only one in there, then guess who is in charge? And, further, guess who can rearrange things if rearrangement is desired? You, and only you, can.

Secondly, not only is all experience inside of us, but it is also always happening right now, because experience can only happen in the present. As a matter of fact, most of us refer to our interior experiencing in terms of *time*:

a) *Thinking*, or consciousness, is NOW experience;

b) The PAST is a current experience of remembered *thought*; and,

c) *Imagination* is creating possible FUTURE experience with current thinking.

Notice that all experience is occurring in the NOW. There really is nothing else but NOW. *Past* and *future* are created in the NOW with *thinking*. Your thinking creates your world - my thinking creates my world. Your thinking changes your world or keeps it the same. My thinking changes my world or keeps it the same. All power is in the NOW. It is simple.

Any single human experience has three "doors" into it. Each experience, no matter how "trivial" or "unnoticed", has <u>physical</u> sensation, <u>mental</u> registration, and <u>emotional</u> evaluation components. We have a tendency to separate them out, when in actuality they are merely *perspectives* of the same experience.

<u>Example:</u>

Consider that you have never seen a fish or an aquarium. You walk into a room where there are three video monitors next to each other. Unbeknown to you, these monitors are connected to three video cameras in another room focused on the same aquarium which contains a single swimming fish. The first camera is focused on the side of the aquarium, the second on the end, and the third is above the aquarium looking straight down on top of the fish. As you gaze at the monitors you believe that three different fish are being monitored. Soon it dawns on you that they are moving in incredible harmony with each other. You deduce that they must have some means of very accurate communication as well as rigorous self-discipline. It is so unbelievable that you focus more and more on the similarities until, in a flash of insight, you realize that they are one in the same fish viewed from three different angles.

So it is with experience. We separate our experience into pieces for reasons of convenience, or out of fear, or from habit, but all pieces are present regardless of our cognizance of them. Success with the Phoenix Solution asks of you to become aware of all three doors into your experiencing of life. The key to the three doors of experience is labeled *awareness* on one side and *willingness* on the other side. You must be *aware* of your physical, emotional, and mental experiential doors, and *willing* to enter and learn from what is behind them.

The Essential Five Steps of The Phoenix Solution

The Phoenix Solution, like all forms of psychotechnology, is a tool. It is a 5-step process designed to create self-determined transformations in your life. The transformations may be major, such as changing your finances, relationships, career, or body, or minor, such as changing your present mood, attitude or outlook. They could even be recreational, such as improving your golf or bowling score, batting average, or swimming skills. It makes no difference, the steps are the same. In order to utilize the Phoenix Solution one needs nothing more than knowledge of the 5-steps and basically what you came into life with: Consciousness and Breath. You don't need electronic devices, tapes, music, special surroundings, or a companion to utilize the Phoenix Solution once you have internalized it. This is truly an independent tool, another reason why it is so empowering. It is you, with all your potential manifested. The Phoenix Solution is the vehicle that moves you in the direction of supreme self-reliance. When you have mastered the Phoenix Solution as described herein, you will carry it conveniently with you forever.

The Phoenix Solution always works if utilized as prescribed. It is already in the most abbreviated form, so please use it exactly as described. When you understand that the Phoenix Solution can replace routines that people have spent years, or even a lifetime, utilizing in an attempt to create transformations in their lives, then you begin to grasp the gravity of what you now hold in your hands, and will soon be using in your daily life.

THE FIVE STEPS OF THE PHOENIX SOLUTION

STEP 1: TRANSFORMING PROBLEMS INTO PASSION
"To change anything, you must first get close."

STEP 2: DEVELOPING THE PROBLEM
"Learn the exact nature of the problem, and who owns it."

STEP 3: PRODUCING THE PRIMARY DOMINO
"Generate the magic formula."

STEP 4: CREATING THE PHOENIX
"A problem is a solution trying to happen."

STEP 5: DOING IT BETTER
"Fine tuning makes the difference."

Each step will be thoroughly described in the following chapters. At the end of each chapter will be seven real examples of people who have utilized the Phoenix Solution on a specific issue in order to create a transformation. You are encouraged to become the eighth person, and experiment with a transformational issue of your own as we go along. Space is provided at the end of each chapter for you to work through a chosen issue step by step.

CHAPTER 7

THE PHOENIX SOLUTION - STEP 1
Passionately Possessing the Problem
A) Emotionally: Willingness - 5 Types
B) Mentally: Responsibility
C) Physically: Conscious Connected Breathing
Seven Truths to Believe In
Real Examples

TRANSFORMING PROBLEMS INTO PASSION

"To change anything, you must first get close..."

Assumption: In order to change something you <u>must</u> own it. You may not know how to actually take ownership, because the natural response to a problem is initially to avoid it. This chapter teaches you how to thoroughly, even passionately, possess a problem.

[Note: A "problem" is defined as *anything you prefer to change.*]

My neighbor across the street painted his house ochre. I hate ochre. I have fantasies about going over there at 2:00 a.m. with a ladder, a brush, and five gallons of blue paint so that when I get up in the morning and face the day it's not an ochre day! But I don't "own" his house, so I cannot really do anything about his actual color choices. I can "own" my attitudes about ochre and change them, or I can make a decision to "own" the way I look out the windows and face a different way when I get up in the morning. I only have power over things I own.

Jim was a raving alcoholic. His relationships with family members were a shambles, his finances were a disaster, his health was failing, and his work performance, on which he always had prided himself, was beginning to slip. His response to these difficulties was to a) blame others, bad luck, the weather, the government, and, b) drink more alcohol. Jim didn't think he had a drinking problem. In other words, he was in a state of *denial*. He could <u>never</u> personally do anything positive about these problems until he consciously began to "own" his situation. He had a long recovery road ahead of him and a casual approach was not about to effectively turn things around. He needed to *passionately possess* his alcoholism to see himself through the lean moments of recovery. This need for passionate possession is why some recovering alcoholics appear addicted to AA meetings for a few years; it is the very fervent attachment they need to sustain sobriety until they have internalized a new alcohol-free life.

In order to gain a foothold on a problem, it must be possessed, and the more significant the problem, the more passionate the possession must be. By not possessing a problem you "disempower" yourself, which sounds a lot like "disemboweling" yourself! Any problem can be overcome if it can first be encircled and embraced. You can never solve your problems by distancing yourself from them. The faster you run, the faster they run. It is with "The buck stops here!" mentality that change effectively begins. Learn this NOW, once and for all. Here's how.

There are three doors to passionate possession of the problem. Your problem is an experience, and it has the three doors corresponding with the three aspects of any experience: emotional, mental, and physical. You can passionately possess a problem utilizing any one of the three doors. Any of the three will work alone...put all three together and the problem doesn't stand a chance!

A) Possessing a problem emotionally

<u>Willingness</u> (preferences/demands)

Change originates within the self because of *willingness*. Without willingness not much changes. This is because humans are made from molecules and are, therefore, somewhat subject to the laws of physics. The Law of Inertia in physics states: "That which is at rest remains at rest until some force operates upon it. Also, that which is in motion remains in motion until some force operates upon it." This means that we have a tendency to keep doing (or not-doing) the same things over and over, <u>until we develop the willingness to change</u>.

The origin of willingness within the mind is difficult to discover since prior to emotional willingness there is just "energy-in-routine," i.e. energy doing nothing but maintaining the status quo. And that is what humans do usually—they just maintain a routine until one type of willingness or another raises its head and provides the impetus for change. It behooves you to understand the different forms of willingness. There are five types of willingness. They are states of mind-emotion and are relatively non-restrictive with regards to age of the person.

WILLINGNESS 1:
The non-judgmental child-like state of mind which is fascinated by and accepting of all sensory input while seeking for connection and exploration.

WILLINGNESS 2:
The state of being in which one is at some level of physical/emotional/mental pain and is in need of specific relief.

WILLINGNESS 3:
A state of advancement in the direction of a predetermined goal in order to experience a sense of progressive movement.

WILLINGNESS 4:
A state of a desire to open up to new combinations of perceived reality due to a sensing of a potential that could be realized.

WILLINGNESS 5:
A wisdomic state of being in which one values positively all that one experiences.

The type of willingness determines not only the type of openness (See Technical Manual), but also the nature of the goal pursued. This implies that attempting to create change with a "growth" inducement (Willingness 3) will not be effective for someone coming from a "discomfort" (Willingness 2) frame of reference. In other words, sometimes the relieving of discomfort is a good motivator for yourself, e.g., "Think how much lighter I will feel when I shed these pounds." At other times, physical discomfort reduction will not work for you, and you may need to say, "When I lose this weight I will know that I can tangibly control something, and then I will have confidence to get even more serious about designing my life the way I want it."

Most adults are motivated by avoidance of painful consequences: "If I don't do _____, something bad will happen." Until they master and feel secure in their lower needs (food, water, warmth, companionship, etc.) people remain stuck with discomfort reduction, or Willingness 2, as a way of life. This is tragically ironic. The development of the capability to permanently master and control the supply of necessities becomes obscured by a constant preoccupation with just the "supply lines." People in this situation are generally so consumed with the necessity of obtaining relief from the <u>demands</u> of stress and insecurity that they often develop blinders to their potential as independently empowered entities. Their constant outward focusing perpetuates an external locus of control, which encourages more outward focusing, ad infinitum.

One way to break this cycle is to base one's desires for change on <u>preferences</u> instead of on <u>demands</u>. It is significantly less stressful to say, "I *prefer* to do the dishes now," as opposed to "I *have* to do the dishes now," or "I *prefer* to have more money," rather than "I've *got to* have more money." This is because the second statement includes desperation and resentment. The first statement is imbued with the freedom to choose and have control over one's life. It is preferable to upgrade your demands to preferences as it places you in an adult to adult relationship with yourself. This is better than a parent-child relationship with yourself based on "shoulds," "havetos," "musts," and "oughtas." These inner negative conversational patterns establish habits of alleviating discomfort with discomforting motivational systems, which will naturally create a need for more alleviation.

<u>Preferences</u> have to do with an individual's desire to change various aspects of experience mentally, emotionally, physically or spiritually. There are many reasons a person may prefer self-designed change. These might include the need to:

a) be better equipped to achieve a goal
b) remove misery from one's life
c) repair damage from the past
d) feel better
e) have more fun
f) be creative
g) be challenged to actualize potentialities
h) increase one's effectiveness
i) lower distress levels
j) give a gift to oneself, another, or society.

It is much easier to launch change from a <u>preferential</u> state than from a <u>demand</u> state. You are encouraged to deliberately up-grade your willingness status from discomfort relief (Willingness 2) to a sense of empowered achievement (Willingness 3). This will lower emotional resistance, alleviate potential distress, and encourage self-responsibility.

B) Possessing a problem mentally

<u>Responsibility</u>

Willingness is an emotionally-dominated door to change. Its mental companion is rational judgment about the advantages of responsibility. One is obviously powerless to change things peacefully without being responsible for them in the first place. If I don't want to be on the Buildings and Grounds committee, then I forfeit my opportunity to decide where the new shrubbery will be placed. If I want to be able to do something about my anger, then it is in my best interest to *own* my anger. If I am uncomfortable with my child's behavior, it is smart to mentally acknowledge my part in co-creating the situation.

Responsibility is an *investment*. To take responsibility for everything that happens in your life is an investment in <u>you</u>. This doesn't mean we don't hold others accountable for their behaviors. It means we definitely hold ourselves accountable for what we do with our life here and now, i.e., if somebody drops a hot potato in your lap, your first "response-ability" should be to take care of yourself. If you lose a body part in an accident caused by another person's carelessness, it is in your best interests to concentrate on <u>what you are going to do with you now</u>. Intellectually it makes sense to be responsible for everything that directly affects you; if you sit with the hot potato in your lap while blaming the culprit, you will have a different future than if you choose instead to make potato salad while waiting for your lawyer to return your call.

TRUTH:
Either you are responsible, or you are a victim, and this <u>is</u> a choice.

Most people don't like the word "responsibility" because as children we never heard it said with a smile. It was always toned as "burdensome" or "heavy" or "laborious." Our poor ancestors carried around that false puritanical thinking, and even felt they were handing us a gift with the attitude: "Suffer big loads of responsibility and someday you will be rewarded." Maybe that half-truth worked well enough to keep them going, but not without a lot of wear and tear, as you probably have observed. The part of the half-truth that is true is that "responsibility is good"; the part of the half-truth that is not true is that "responsibility should be a burden."

Another TRUTH:
Responsibility is the key to liberation.

Again, you have no control over modifying that for which you are not responsible. Having no responsibility over a situation is akin to being a victim in that particular situation. This book is mostly concerned with your internal state from which all things flow (or don't flow) for you. When speaking of responsibility know that it begins within, even if the observable results of responsible behavior are seen without.

Responsibility begins with thought. So let's have a new thinking about responsibility. No matter who or what you have been blaming for your condition, your problems, your emotions, your whatever, up until now, rest assured that it is in your best interest to believe the following thinking from now on:

"I love everything about being responsible for everything I experience or refrain from experiencing!"

It is important to memorize this and think it to yourself 20 times a day no matter how much you currently dispute it. After a few days (or minutes if you are a fast learner), when you see the truth and power of this thinking, you will have a wonderful experience of empowerment. You won't need to repeat it anymore because you will **know** it to be true. If you still have trouble accepting it, write it out ten times a day. When you "get it" you will smile or laugh. This realization alone is worth a fortune, and without this realization few vital things are going to happen by design in your life.

A special note: This affirmative form of thinking is not to induce guilt, as does the belief, "I have cancer and I created it in myself." Affirmations are used to induce empowerment, for example, "I now own this cancer and I can do something about it!" It is difficult to do anything about something if you don't own it. You are stuck with the color your neighbor paints his house, but you can choose not to look at it or talk about it. When we discuss responsibility, we are not talking about **revenge** as some do when they attempt to decide who "the responsible party" was, or unresolved anger expressing itself as **resentment** when we say, "Aha, you are the one who was responsible," or **righteousness**, "It wasn't my fault!", or the flipside of righteousness, **regret** (guilt), "Oh, [sob] it was my fault." Let us be clear on this: We are discussing who is going to own your life. It is a business-like decision. Are you or aren't you going to own, direct, produce and star in your own life?

And yet another TRUTH:
Either you are responsible, or you are responsible for being irresponsible.

Now wouldn't you just know it—there is no escaping responsibility! Even if you have been victimized (and people do not always "create" that in their lives as some say!) you are responsible with what you are going to do with that incident.

And still yet another TRUTH:
All woundings are not self-inflicted, but all healings are.

Some victims are not aware that they self-fertilize their own victimization through self-pity, self-inflicted reenactments, denial, the four R's (revenge, resentment, righteousness and regret), or unwillingness to pursue healing. The Phoenix Solution is designed to facilitate your overcoming all these reasons for staying in misery.

Big TRUTH:
Responsibility is empowering, and the more of it you have, the more you have of what you want.

If you choose not to own something, you lose the right to change it. Convinced?

C) Possessing a problem physically

Conscious Connected Breathing (CCB)

True passion is not just thought or emotion; it consumes the body with total involvement. The reason some people are afraid of passion is that they fear the feeling of losing themselves. This, of course, is correct in the sense that they are never going to be the same after being immersed in something that is as overwhelming as passion. On the other hand, if what is lost is a passionless existence, then what is lost isn't much worth preserving anyway, now is it?

Even if <u>emotionally</u> you are unwilling to possess the problem, and <u>mentally</u> you feel unable to assume responsibility for the problem, and are, as a result, still blocked from possessing the problem, there is one surefire method for taking ownership.

VERY IMPORTANT NOTE: Breathing is central to life and Conscious Connected Breathing is central to the efficacy of The Phoenix Solution. Learn the following well by using it often. It has many, many benefits.

DO THIS:
Keep your breathing circular
...connecting the inhale and exhale...
*As you read this take in a slow full breath
...a little more...
...and a little more still...
Gently and slowly, that's it...
Now, after your chest is fairly full...
Let go of your breath so that your chest slowly goes down...
Refrain from controlling the exhale in any way...
...just let the exhale come out by itself...
When your chest is almost empty
go back to the * in the italicized part of this
paragraph and do it again nine more times.
(Yes, nine more times.)

Notice how you feel differently after doing this just ten times. Whatever you are feeling you are feeling *different*, aren't you? Just ten consciously connected breaths with a relaxed exhale, provides a noticeable shift. That *difference* can also be called *acceptance*, because this is the way you breathe when you are in a happy/serene/peaceful frame of mind, i.e., "accepting what is so." The reason CCB is so powerful is that it allows you to accept situations your mind usually rejects, thus overcoming a major roadblock in terms of influencing that situation. Note that "accepting" something is not the same as "affirming" something: *Acceptance* encircles something so that you can change it if you prefer, and *affirmation* means that you like something just the way it is. For example, I can accept that you smoke cigarettes (I know you must really <u>need</u> them or you wouldn't be doing this to yourself!), although I prefer you to change. If I <u>affirm</u> your smoking, I believe it's a great idea for you to do this to yourself! Again, the advantage of accepting something you would normally reject gives you control over how it is going to influence you. If you reject anything, you have no choice but to run from it, either until you learn to accept it, or until you fall into a grave.

Although it is so familiar to you, breathing is very different from other body functions. It is a body function that happens automatically or can be done with deliberate consciousness. Heartbeats, digestion, circulatory functions, body temperature regulation, neural transmissions, etc. are difficult to take over and perform consciously. Breathing, on the other hand, can be taken over in the blink of an eye and, in this case, used to your definite advantage—the advantage of always being at *choice* rather than being at *no-choice*.

TRUTH:
In order to effectively change anything by deliberate self-design, one must always come from the position of choice.

One of the primary signs of life is whether you are breathing or not. Breath is more significant in your life than water, sunlight or food. If you need proof, ask yourself this question: "Of breath, water, sunlight or food, which am I willing to go an hour without?" Breathing has another significant function; it is a barometer monitored by your brain in an ongoing evaluation of your current life situation. When you feel threatened you hold your breath or breathe shallowly. Notice the way you breathe the next time you balance your checkbook! On the other hand, when we feel at peace, as when watching a beautiful sunset or experiencing "afterglow," we breathe fully and slowly. Because you can make a conscious choice to change your breathing pattern to benefit you, and since the autonomic nervous system reads your body language, especially your mode of breathing, to see if there is cause for alarm (and need for subsequent fight or flight tension), *it is in your best interests to breathe slowly and fully as often as you remember to do so.*

Slow and full breathing sends a physiological message of serenity to your muscles, circulatory system and glands, even if you <u>are</u> in a stressful situation. Most of us have grown up succumbing to a natural reaction of contracting our breathing again and again in response to fearful conditions and, upon reaching adulthood, have developed a habit pattern of shallow broken breathing <u>which sends a constant message of panic</u> to the blind autonomic nervous system.

Conscious connected breathing restores your physical-emotional-mental state to that of a baby-at-peace...like you used to be...while empowering you at the same time. This last statement will certainly challenge any of you who are still carrying around the notion that being perpetually tense and hypervigilant keeps you in control and safe. It doesn't (don't you have enough proof by now?) because being tense and hypervigilant is a *victim stance*, and invites perpetrators like blood in the water attracts sharks. Let me assure you that you are very well-equipped to respond to an emergency from a relaxed CCB state. Just like my gray Persian cat, who <u>never</u> uses the kitty barbells I bought her, can change from a totally limp posture into an instant lightning bolt of action at the mere hint of a mouse sighting, you too can go from a relaxed state to instant action if needed.

Conscious Connected Breathing (CCB) Guidelines

1) Connect the inhale and exhale "at both ends," keeping the breathing totally circular. Sometimes it helps to have a visual image inside your head. Some people use a thought-picture of a connected white string going from the external environment into the lungs and back out again. One person thought of bicycle pedals going round and round. Some see connected arrows.

2) Relax the exhale, refraining from controlling the exhale with the stomach, chest, throat or lips. *Just let the air exit of its own accord.* Surprisingly, this may take concentrated practice. Discovering just how much you have been conditioned over the

years to eke out your exhale can be a real eye-opener. Practice until the exhale is naturally easy and free.

DO THIS: Stack up your vertebrae and close your eyes (after you read this) and breathe fully and connectedly for five minutes.

Notice after about thirty seconds (when you begin to feel good) how your mind wants you to get busy with something else. This is an example of how we like to rain on our own parade!

3) If you experience uncomfortable dizziness the first few times you do CCB, don't take in quite so much air. If you like being dizzy, then breathe deeper.

4) Do CCB whenever you think of it. Good times to practice are while waiting in line or at a railroad crossing. Utilize CCB during times of tension when you feel out of control, such as when getting a speeding ticket, interviewing for a new job, facing your boss, arguing with your (or anybody else's) spouse, or worrying about anything in the universe.

5) CCB is a terrific way to control insomnia. By merely relaxing and doing slow-and-full conscious connected breathing, you will drift off to sleep or, at the very least, you will feel so peaceful you won't care if you remain awake.

6) CCB is a great way to start your day. Arise five minutes earlier than usual, sit on the floor or in a chair with your back straight, and do 5 minutes of conscious connected breathing. Notice the difference in your morning!

7) Slow and full breathing is the most peaceful. If you are filled with fear or anger and cannot seem to hold a lot of air, still keep

your breathing connected until you can breathe more deeply; then do so for at least five minutes to help resolve the previous episode.

8) Practicing and playing with CCB over time will prove to you what a natural power source you possess 24 hours a day. It can become your way of being a constantly nurturing and empowering companion to yourself.

Step 1 Summary

Step 1 gives three methods for owning a problem. When you determine that something needs changing <u>that</u> is a problem. Life is full of problems. Life may even <u>be</u> problems. One thing is certain: You are unable to do anything about a problem if you don't know how to make it part of your reality by getting close.

SUMMARY TRUTH:
The more positively and passionately you accept a problem as part of your reality, the more power you possess for changing it.

The degree to which one is effective at problem-solving is not only related to acceptance, but also to the enthusiasm of that acceptance. Enthusiasm has to do with the magnitude of acceptance physically, emotionally and mentally. Basically, enthusiasm is willingness, responsibility and Conscious Connected Breathing on a rheostat. The more you turn these three up at any moment the more enthused you will feel in that moment.

Yet another TRUTH:
Your only choice at any one moment is to passionately possess what is happening in the NOW, or to procrastinate doing so---it is always up to you, and only you.

This and the next four chapters each cover a phase of the Phoenix Solution. To facilitate absorption of this powerful vehicle for change, actual examples from real life will be given at the end of each of these chapters to illustrate the progressive utilization of the Phoenix Solution. [Names have been changed to preserve anonymity.] Please select a problem of your own that you have not yet resolved and experiment along as person #8. Write in your name and then journal through each of the five steps.

Phoenix Solution/Step 1 - Real Examples

Terry Doubleton: Terry is definitely an above average golfer. But he has reached that plateau that is so familiar in most sports, where you just don't seem to get any better no matter how much you practice. Every year at the beginning of the season he rustily starts out about 10 over par and then in about a month gets down to his usual 6 handicap. But this year is to be an exception, because he has learned of the Phoenix Solution. At first he had, as most people do, misidentified his problem by thinking he just wasn't trying hard enough. His customary solution was to practice more, concentrate on every move more, swing harder, get angry when it didn't work and then try harder some more. This time he decides to back off from the pressure approach and just focus on the differences in his thought processes on days he does well and days he doesn't. Implicit ownership of the problem is achieved by surrendering his old strategy of blaming his clubs and anything else in the universe for his inability to reduce his golf score and by doing conscious connected breathing (CCB). Patient objective observation of himself becomes his strategy instead.

William Foxworthy: Bill is ten years into his marriage and his wife, Madeline, is telling him that he isn't the man she married. Madeline says that Bill is insensitive, distant, and "letting himself go." Bill complains that Madeline is a nag, doesn't want sex anymore, and that he's too tired to exercise after working all the time to 'make a good home' for Madeline and the kids. End result: Bill has not done anything about the problem. He is reluctant, but decides to apply the Phoenix Solution anyway. Emotionally, Bill is in the "arm-twisting" state of willingness, but he has decided that avoidance isn't fixing anything so he takes the reins and decides to apply the Phoenix Solution. As Bill does more and more CCB, he begins to feel better and more passionate about the responsibility he is assuming, finally deciding to do something about an ongoing uncomfortable situation in his life.

Susan Purnell: Sue has always had difficulty with trusting others. She doesn't remember that she was sexually abused as a small child, but it has shown up in a series of broken relationships. Right now she lives alone, is divorced, and is exhausted because of recurring nightmares she has about being suffocated. She thinks there is something intrinsically wrong with her, and is, therefore, in possession of the problem, although for an inaccurate reason. She is more than willing to perform CCB because it helps her relax and even sleep better.

Gwendolyn Smith-Burnett: Gwen has been sick for over a year and has gone through many months of grueling and expensive medical tests with no answers forthcoming for her nausea and dizziness. She continues to look for an 'out there' cause that could be nullified by medication, thus restoring her health. She wonders if the doctors believe it is all "in her head." Out of desperation and frustration she takes ownership, focuses internally, and begins to breathe and relax into her symptoms.

David Birnbaum: Dave is a hardware salesman and a runner who is well-versed in the Phoenix Solution. While running today he gets a painful stitch in his side and instantly embraces it with CCB.

Elizabeth Rohrbach: Liz is a mother and Avon sales lady who has been through a Psychotechnology Seminar and utilizes the Phoenix Solution many times daily to direct her life through changes she desires. Right now she is in a bad mood and wants to change it. First, she skips the "Why am I in a bad mood?" delay tactic and begins CCB immediately and enthusiastically. She enjoys the power and adventure of being able to change her life in any way she chooses.

Christina Ishtar: Christina is a 46 year old woman thoroughly trained in a number of spiritual disciplines who has reached solutions to many life challenges. A problem she has been unable to address confidently is her weight. For many years she has considered herself "slightly overweight." However, in the past two years since her father's death, the weight gain has escalated. She now considers herself significantly overweight and is very unhappy. She is experiencing constant indigestion and chest pain, just like Daddy used to. Meditation helps her be more at peace with the problem, but she continues to gain. Eating plans, starving, diet pills, diet beverages, and exercise have proven to be only temporary solutions. As soon as she feels deprived, her resolve weakens and she regains the weight. She feels a failure at maintaining a healthy weight and decides to try the Phoenix Solution, partly to see if it will work and partly driven by the fear of being "fat and fifty."

You:

A) Problem to be possessed:
_____
_____
_____
_____

B) Describe your level of willingness: (See pages 55-56 and/or Technical Manual section)
_____
_____

C) Begin Conscious Connected Breathing.

D) Reflect on what you have written in A & B and modify them if necessary.

E) CCB some more and say to yourself, "I own this problem. It is mine, all mine."

F) Allow yourself to own the problem physically and emotionally as well as mentally.

CHAPTER 8

THE PHOENIX SOLUTION - STEP 2
Understanding the Problem
Six Dynamics of Problems
A) Problem Identification: Assessing the Situation
3 Blocks to Accurate Assessment
B) Expanding the Number of Possible Explanations
The Powerful Listing Method
C) Selecting the Most Accurate Explanation
Five Truths to Believe In
Real Examples

DEVELOPING THE PROBLEM

"Learn the exact nature of the problem, and determine who really owns it."

Problems that are correctly assessed do not remain problems for very long. If a problem hangs around for awhile, it's a good bet that it has been inaccurately assessed. As a psychotherapist I learned quite a few things about problems.

<u>Six Dynamics of Problems</u>

1) If a client "knew" on our first meeting what the problem was, then more than likely the problem wasn't that. So, for now, figure that whatever issues have been bothering you for some time have probably been misdiagnosed.

2) This is usually true because a correctly stated problem has a built-in solution and people, being smart, will immediately take steps to solve the problem, e.g., "I'm hungry because it has been five hours since I have eaten food. Solution: Eat some food." For many clients, once the problem was clarified <u>our</u> work was

finished, and they went off clearly and confidently to do what they knew had to be done.

3) People often identify problems correctly but misidentify the true owner of the problem, e.g., "It drives me nuts when your room is a mess...what's wrong with <u>you</u>!" It does make you feel and even appear less than sane when you are trying to own and solve somebody else's problem...and this is a <u>very</u> <u>common</u> dilemma.

Chad had a female friend with compulsive behaviors that he kept trying to fix by pointing out her problems, giving her articles to read, arguing with her, manipulating situations, and even speaking with professionals on her behalf. Her compulsions worsened, so his response was to redouble his efforts. This strategy created even more compulsive energy until the woman was eventually spending over 8 hours a day in her behavior. He identified "his problem" as her behavior, which left him no recourse but to continue his unsuccessful efforts at controlling her. Against both their desires, the relationship, due to overwhelming frustration, wound up as an abusive one. At issue was: To whom does her problem behavior belong? The answer was apparent: her behavior was her issue and hers alone. His problem was ignorance in knowing how to associate with a loved one burdened by compulsive behaviors. Once this realization became internalized by each of them, they were free to concentrate their energies on solutions that would really work.

4) Life provides an abundance of challenges called 'problems.' The quest in life is not to run out of problems, but to replace nit-picky problems with big juicy ones that let you know you are getting somewhere when you solve them! To constantly worry over the same rent payment every month is a nit-picky problem that is endless, with only a temporary reprieve at best. Every time you "solve" this problem by finally paying the rent, your mind knows that the problem truly has not gone away, but is just

hibernating for a few weeks. A nice juicy problem is to raise your level of income by getting a college education or embarking on a new job search; this produces a sense of "mission" which feels much more productive despite the added pressures of shifting a lot of new gears.

5) All problems can be solved if you are willing to: a) assess them accurately (including discovering ownership); b) chunk down the solution into right-size pieces; and c) be persistent in applying solutions. This includes attempts at changing life situations or personal characteristics.

6) The major internal blocks to solving problems boil down to just two: Ignorance and Stubbornness. Either a person doesn't have enough knowledge about the problem to be solved, or when the needed knowledge is obtained, the person is unyielding in their old patterns and refuses to apply what is known. Many humans are more concerned with being *right* about not changing destructive patterns than being healthy and happy. Strange as it may seem, people often die rather than change, a disease known as "terminal righteousness." Don't be one of those.

A) Problem Identification: Assessing the situation

The assessment phase is where precision begins to play a critical role in the deliberate self-design process. If the key area of concern cannot be accurately pinpointed, one is left with an ineffective strategy akin to shooting at noises in the dark, or, worse still, shooting at the wrong target in the light. These strategies of random-shooting and wrong-targeting are, of course, the most often used approaches to problem-solving. This explains why many problems are never satisfactorily solved. One can only begin to wonder if there isn't a hidden investment in *non-solution* in these cases. Parents who continually find things to criticize in their children may have a need to have power over something they can control, so it really doesn't matter how much the kids improve. There will be no end to the criticism. The *source* of the tirades may be the real problem and not the child's spotlighted behavior.

TRUTH:
You won't discover the source of light by following the beam to where it is pointing.

A graduate program at a small college in Iowa could not understand why they didn't get their fair share of the college's marketing budget. Month after month they blamed themselves for not presenting a good case to administration, or they blamed the publicity director (the college president's right-hand man) for being prejudiced against the graduate division; as their enrollment began to dwindle, they also blamed other colleges for cutting into their territory. Crazy feelings and criticism abounded until three years later it was uncovered that the college president had a secret clause in his contract that he received a yearly bonus which was based, not on total enrollment figures, but on undergraduate enrollment only. Suddenly the problem was clear. It was now obvious why the graduate program was not mentioned in general college advertising and publicity releases and received so little coverage in campus newspapers and magazines mailed out to the public. Once the problem was correctly assessed, the graduate division began altering their attack on the problem by convincing the president that the graduate program's success would increase the attractiveness of the school to potential undergraduate enrollees. Almost miraculously, many of the graduate program's marketing concerns began moving toward resolution.

In Step 1 you must assume possession of a problem passionately to get close enough to determine the true ownership of the problem. Upon further investigation in Step 2 it may be discovered that one actually does not own the problem formerly possessed in Step 1. Therein lies the shortcut solution known as "giving it back." Giving it back is mostly mental relief in the security of once and for all knowing that it truly isn't your problem. This allows you to lift the burden from your shoulders and to walk away free of the necessity of finding a solution. You can also formally give it back by informing someone that "This is not my problem." If you have to live or work with that person, then you may experience Chad's challenge, learning to live with someone who has a problem and doesn't take care of it. This is much, much easier to do than trying to solve a problem that isn't yours!

Three Blocks to Accurate Assessment

It is of such importance to get off on the right foot in diagnosing a problem, that it is in your best interests to closely examine some reasons for potential difficulty in doing just that. As you read along, it is helpful to verify these points by remembering real examples from your own experiences.

1) <u>Dishonesty as a Block to Accurate Assessment</u>

Integrity is rare. Lack of integrity (inaccurate disclosure) exists because of fear-filled childhood experiences of being punished for being honest. The fear of disclosure became based upon a belief that "If the truth be known, I will suffer pain in some form." By the time humans have reached adulthood they have seen ample proof of this and have evolved elaborate schemes to fool others and themselves.

It is unfortunate that children often get punished for just being themselves. All child abuse and neglect is received by children as a message that "You are not good enough the way you are." A child's fear and/or willingness to please is their first sacrifice of integrity: "I shall pretend to *be* (think/feel/do) someone I am not." And they are reinforced in this strategy by the subsequent withdrawal of the punishment or even by being rewarded with a smile, a goody, or a loving touch, thus imbedding the strategy of sacrificing integrity for the sake of relieving pain or gaining reward. It worked then, it may have even been the way to stay alive, and it still works for adults treating each other and themselves like children. But nothing works as well as honesty.

TRUTH:
Now that I am an adult I can lay aside old childhood strategies for surviving and being loved, and I will be safe.

Oh, you may get a few raised eyebrows simply because people will notice a change in you, but I haven't heard of anyone getting killed by a raised eyebrow since back in '09! The message here is that we must exhibit the same Step 1 willingness we utilized to passionately possess the problem, to now answer the question: "Honestly, just what is the real problem here?" and refuse to accept our own snappy answers. Remember, if you instantly feel you have the answer to an ongoing problem, that's probably not the answer. Be willing to get even more honest, and more honest still.

2) Non-focusing as a Block to Accurate Assessment

Yes, the usual strategy for dealing with a problem is best described as "running like hell." Unfortunately problems have a way of running as fast as your shadow, so this strategy has largely proven ineffective. Good assessment mandates a willingness to *focus* on the problem...to be *with* the problem...to get close enough to the problem to notice how it ticks. This means rejecting avoidance strategies such as ignoring, daydreaming, fantasizing, changing the subject, quick judgment dispensation, medicating with ingestion of food/alcohol/nicotine/drugs/etc., "problem-hopping," or compulsive habits. Instead, sit quietly with an assessment mentality while doing Conscious Connected Breathing and you will eventually know what you need to know.

TRUTH:
Peel the onion to the core and there will be no more tears or fears.

3) <u>Not Enough Information as a Block to Accurate Assessment</u>

You are limited (*limit* = how far you let yourself go) to the extent of the information you have available to you at any one moment. Herein lies the intrinsic worth of true education: It gives an individual more choices. Ignorance in a particular situation means a lack of internal tools and skills (information and processes) to modify that situation. It is in your best interest to have enough humility (knowing your current limits) and willingness to continually expand your knowledge base. "Problems" present the opportunity and motivation to do just this...a good enough reason to be grateful for the next problem you get! Each problem solved expands your holdings and your chances for success in the next problem arena, and so on and so on, exponentially.

In other words, sometimes it behooves you to <u>learn</u>, in the classic sense, about a problem by reading, asking, pondering, researching, digging, and absorbing. Not to worry: If you don't have the necessary motivation to seek out new information, Step 4 will often create that drive in you.

<u>A practice session with assessment</u>

In this practice session you are going to play with assessment. Eventually you will be adept at doing this quickly, but for right now absorb it one step at a time. For this exercise we will define "problem" as *anything which one is challenged in changing.* As an example, if I notice I am thirsty, that is not a problem although it is a situation calling for change. If I am thirsty and I am unable to find water, <u>that</u> is a problem because it is a potentially difficult challenge. Decisions are not problems (unless you have a problem making decisions.)

DO THIS: Sit straight up in a quiet place and do one minute of CCB. Relax your body and your thinking...just let everything *be*. After one minute or so, when you feel open to exploration, spend a little time selecting a problem in your personal life that you would like to change (not the same one you are using at the end of the Step chapters). Clearly focus on the problem and make it as real as you can in your mind. This is called *bringing definition to the problem*. Now as you breathe connectedly with a relaxed exhale ask yourself this question: "Who really owns this problem?" [ALWAYS contemplate for at least 10 seconds prior to answering!]

If the answer is someone other than yourself go to i) below.

If the answer is, "I own this problem." go to ii) below.

i) Continue the process along with the CCB and relaxation: "What does taking on someone else's problem have to offer me?" Be ruthless in listening for all the answers you will hear—and there can be many, so hear them all. Some will be weird, some will seem silly, some will not please you, but the objective here is to provide an audience for them all.

If after hearing the answers, you see that you have no interest in continuing possessing other people's problems in futility, decide how you are going to "give back" the problem (which was never yours in the first place!) Then make a commitment to do that, with a definitive time by which it will be done. If you are still unable to let go of someone's problem, then your problem can be defined as "meddling" in other people's problems and you can use that as your problem.

ii) Now ask yourself, "What do I gain by having this problem?" Again be willing to hear all the answers no matter how unusual they may be, and be willing to own them all no matter how they make you feel. This is called *ownership of the problem*.

[So, lest you be confused: Back in Step 1 you passionately possess a problem long enough to find out in Step 2 whether you actually do own it or were incorrect in believing you did. Sometimes you passionately possess a problem just long enough to find out it isn't yours.]

Realize that in order to be effective with the Phoenix Solution, you need flexibility and a general refraining from "hair-trigger assessments" involving snappy ego-driven explanations and solutions. The need to be right is inherent in all of us, and that is not only good but necessary for survival. But when we are stubbornly insistent on "being right," we will soon fall victim to our own ego—and it will be, without a doubt, painful and confusing. Have enough humility from the beginning to suspend judgment until you have taken in the whole scene. You have everything to gain by having a little patience.

B) Problem Identification: Expanding the number of possible explanations

It is interestingly tragic how people can be so snappy with solutions that do not work and how slow they can be to realize this. Sadly, many proposed "solutions" are actually just poor attempts at explanation. These poor explanations become futile attempts to solve a dilemma. For example,

a) "I don't feel good about my weight—but I just can't stop eating."
b) "I can't find peace—my kids drive me crazy."
c) "My business is not doing well—the employees are not working hard enough."

Notice how externally located the implied solutions are in these explanations.
a) Food controls how I feel.
b) The kids are in charge of how peaceful I can feel.
c) My employees are in control of the success of my business.

If you locate potential cures for your problems "out there," the results are usually zero. Problems are usually not "out there" and, if they are, the solution is generally obvious and once applied begets immediate and long lasting results.

BIG TRUTH:
Problems are located within.

Believing anything other than this is a disowning of the problem. Disowning the problem leaves one powerless to do anything reasonable and workable about it. No wonder people acting to solve their problems on the basis of constant misdiagnosis begin to feel, and even appear, nutty. For a good graphic representation of this, imagine what would happen if you dropped an anvil on your foot but for some reason located the pain in your right ear. There you are hobbling around looking for ear drops and/or treatment for your ear, trying to convince everyone (and yourself) that there really is a problem with your ear. Can you relate this to something in your life?

You say, "But some problems really are 'out there.' If a car breaks down, **it** is causing me a problem and I get angry." Your statement is that *car breakdowns upset me*, which is simply not true. The next time you are driving somewhere and you see someone at the side of the road with a stalled car, notice that you are probably not upset!

"Upsets" are emotions which arise from challenging circumstances. They are created by two things: a) a violation of our expectations; and b) a remembrance of unfinished business from our past, both of which we own! In other words, you cannot upset me, only I can upset me by my expectations (which I can control, if I so choose), or by my history (which is all mine and can be healed, if I so choose. See *Resolving Unfinished Business* in Bibliography). It is an incredibly liberating thought to know that you (and only you) can control all of your upsets.

A special note on boundaries

Humans are supposed to develop a concept of *boundary*, an immediate territory around themselves that they reside in, maintain, and control. At birth we didn't have a good sense of boundary as we couldn't take care of ourselves. We had to rely on others who were supposed to maintain and control us *for a while* until we took control of ourselves. Since everyone around us was bigger, more experienced and more powerful, we let them have their way. Our other choice was to die.

Nurturing and intelligent caregivers facilitate their children's development of a sense of independence and healthy self-maintenance as they grow older. As adults, children raised in this manner are capable of not only running their lives successfully but also raising their offspring likewise. This implies that a healthy child gradually develops a set of internal tools and external skills in order to operate with stability inside their boundaries and to interact meaningfully outside of them. Unfortunately, for many of us this was not the case. Even from the best of homes we were conditioned codependently to trust others or things - luck, fate, nature, deities - more than ourselves, and we never fully actualized our true independence which is our birthright. We learned enough to get by, and get by we do, but just getting by is not our destiny.

TRUTH:
Those who live to just get by never realize their destiny to fly.

Understandably many humans have chosen to just get by <u>and that is their right</u>. We always have the choice of living below our potential. Another choice is to move in the direction of realizing our potential. If we choose the latter, it mandates that we locate the source of our problems inside ourselves. With all this in mind, let us return to our quest for *expanding the realm of possible explanations,* limiting ourselves to changes possible within our own system of thinking.

Unless one quickly and accurately assesses the root cause of a problem (in which case you can skip Step 2 and go right to Step 3) it is essential to suspend judgment long enough to do some reflective thinking, which is what the old "Count to 10" adage was all about. So know that the first step in contemplation is restraint—restraint from reaching a "quick and dirty" answer until all the possibilities are in. But, if after 'restraining' for a while, no explanation yet makes sense, then more drastic measures are necessary! Get out a pencil and a piece of paper.

The Listing Method

Write the problem at the top of a sheet of paper. State it as clearly and specifically as you can. Then, while performing CCB, write 20 reasons, as quickly as you can why this problem might exist. Don't think or hesitate, just write anything no matter how crazy or funny it may sound to you. This process gets you past your mental blocks that keep you from the truth.

Example: I can't stop eating candy.
1) I love it!
2) It makes me feel good.
3) I deserve it.
4) I was never allowed to eat it when I was a child.
5) It prevents boredom.
6) It gives me energy.
7) It helps me to forget things because it keeps me busy.
8) It keeps me from being successful in my desire to be trim.
9) I get to shop for it.
10) It's a way of rewarding myself.

11) Nobody can tell me when and how much I get to eat it.
12) It curbs my appetite.
13) It gives me another excuse to hate myself.
14) It's MINE, all MINE (I don't have to share it with anybody).
15) It brings out the little kid in me.
16) It brings back fond memories.
17) I just have a sweet tooth.
18) It's my private stroke to myself.
19) I'm addicted to it.
20) Rebellion: It proves that I can eat anything I want!

Step 2 C) Problem Identification: Select the most accurate of the explanations

Perhaps there was an "aha!" experience even when you were doing The Listing Method. If so, then this would move you into Step 3. If you did not have the "aha," then do the listing again with different answers and this time really push it outlandishly, and don't forget to breathe. If this didn't provide the "aha," look over what you have written so far and, while CCBing, select the one that is most meaningful to you. You are ready for Step 3.

Phoenix Solution/Step 2 - Real Examples

Terry Doubleton: Instead of being blinded by frustration with his unsuccessful attempts to improve his golf game, Terry's strategy of patient observation of his better days vs. his worse days begins to pay off. It dawns on him that the days he leaves his high pressure job to play golf he doesn't play as well as when he plays on a Saturday or holiday when he is not coming from a pressure situation. Similarly, if he and his wife have had an argument before he leaves for the club, he doesn't play as well. At first he blames his job and his wife. But then, reminding himself of the benefits of ownership, he focuses his attention on how pressure affects him. Particularly, Terry notices his long ball game suffers on these days more than anything else.

William Foxworthy: Bill initially assessed the situation with his wife, Madeline, as being basically "her fault." Bill, being an intelligent man, realizes that the Blaming Method for problem-solving brings him no closer to an answer for the discomfort in his marital life, so he begins to examine other potential explanations. After rejecting a number of emotionally-laden and defensive possibilities, such as "Women are nags," "I'm unattractive," "Life sucks," Bill realizes that things in the marriage have indeed changed, and not necessarily with any planning or agreement. Bill and his wife have just drifted into what amounted to a breach of contract from what they had originally decided they wanted out of life when they were in the process of dating and becoming a couple. Bill and Madeline are deeply angry and feel "ripped-off" by what has happened, supposedly without their permission, and they are taking it out on each other.

Bill looks at his situation and begins to realize that due to long-term neglect there is more than one issue in the relationship that needs addressing. His weight is an issue, as is his need for exercise, his workaholic attitude, sex in the marriage, and, of course, communication problems in the relationship. All of these issues are important, and Bill decides to attack them one by one. For many reasons he decides to begin an exercise program of walking an hour a day. He feels this will help him lose weight, be healthier, remove him from work for at least an hour a day, and give him a chance to reflect on his life. Walking will also provide him with one hour a day to apply the Phoenix Solution to his issues, and do CCB without interruptions—and it just might help his sex life too! He is immediately met with internal resistance to his own best idea (Comfort Zone Violation!) and begins to realize just how deeply attached he is to his "problems." Being aware of the need to risk the comfort zone violation, Bill intuits that a walking exercise program is still the best breaker of his boycott against his own betterment. How to do it, is the question?

Susan Purnell: As her insomnia is not going away, Susan decides to take a more proactive stance, first by assessing the problem. She initially will misdiagnose her problems as a sleeping disorder ("nightmares") and a relationship problem ("all men are alike"), but this is okay as long as she begins somewhere and then continues following the Phoenix Solution steps. Susan intuits that the reason she is exhausted is because of the disturbing dream of suffocation.

Gwendolyn Smith-Burnett: With the willingness to take ownership of her illness, Gwen begins to notice slight patterns in her illness. She is actually nauseous and dizzy 24 hours a day but sometimes she is more nauseous than others. She starts a journal and perceives that she is much more ill after consuming dairy products. Gwen goes to the library, checks out six books and begins to learn about dairy intolerance. As the symptomology looks very familiar, she intuits that she must eliminate all dairy products from her diet in order to discover if that is indeed her problem.

David Birnbaum: The stitch is David's side is increasing in intensity as he runs. So, while continuing to do CCB he looks at all the possibilities: stop running; slow down; run faster; maintain speed but attempt internal modification. David decides on the last option.

Elizabeth Rohrbach: Beth quickly assesses potential causes of her bad mood to determine if it is an indicator of something she should take care of right away: Did she eat something that disagrees with her?; Is there someone in her environment that she needs to confront?; Did something happen that consciously reminds her of old unfinished business? etc., and she finds no evidence of a simple cause-effect relationship that needs addressing. Knowing better than to spend an inordinate amount of time on "Why...?" questions she quickly takes aim at direct mood modification.

Christina Ishtar: Christina has kept a journal for many years. She reads through old journals to see how she has identified the problem in the past. She finds she has blamed her roommate, who loves junk food and encourages her to eat between meals. She has blamed her friends who constantly tell her she is not fat. She has blamed her Southern upbringing for attracting her to unhealthy, high-fat foods. She has blamed her family because her mother withheld food as punishment, and also meals were often interrupted by family fights. She has blamed her genes because most of her family was or is fat. She has blamed middle age because it is said to be more difficult to lose weight after 40.

After recognizing her preliminary blaming behavior, Christina uses CCB and the Listing Method to find out where her responsibility lies. Her "aha" reaction reveals that the extra weight indicates a misplaced need for love. In order to fit in and be accepted by her fat family, she feels she must be fat. She also feels very deprived of love by her father's death, and feels that if she were as fat as her late father, perhaps her mother would love her more, or at least feel sorry for her.

Realizing that this too is a form of blaming, Christina makes a decision to love herself enough to maintain a healthy weight, giving herself a healthy body as a gift. She begins feeling attracted to magazine articles about healthy eating. Several articles recommend eating 5-7 servings of fruits and vegetables a day. She decides that, in order to not feel deprived, she can eat anything she wants, as long as she eats the 5-7 servings of fruits and vegetables as well.

You:
Do the practice session with assessment on page 77.

Perform the listing method on your problem on page 82.

Select the most accurate explanation of your chosen problem from the listing method and write it here:

_____
_____
_____
_____

CHAPTER 9

THE PHOENIX SOLUTION - STEP 3
Formulating the Answer
Simplifying the Problem into a Modifier Statement
Seven Guidelines for Great Modifiers
Shaping the Modifier into a Primary Domino Thought
Attaching a Timer
Real Examples

PRODUCING THE PRIMARY DOMINO

"Generate the magic formula."

Formulation

Step 3 is also known as the *formulation phase*. Don't let that scare you with its technological ring. It just means that in Step 3 you are going to design a shorter version of the problem explanation you derived in Step 2. We call this shorter version the *modifier* and the process of creating that modifier is called *formulation*. The *modifier* is very important. It is, in effect, the primary agent of change in the Phoenix Solution. Considering the *modifier's* importance, obviously the process of developing it deserves special attention. Are you starting to feel like a scientist? In effect, you <u>are</u> becoming a scientist experimenting with yourself. Enter into it with that spirit, and see what you discover in this wonderful laboratory you call "me."

Step 3. A) Converting the selected problem explanation into a Modifier

A simple but essential conversion is called for once the most accurate explanation for a particular problem has been arrived at in Step 2. The conversion is similar to the preparation of food for assimilation into the body. We do this through *digestion*, a series of food transformations starting with chewing and swallowing. The conversion from a Step 2 Problem Explanation to the development of a Step 3 *modifier* is known as *formulation* and consists of rephrasing the explanation into a proactive positive solution statement. If, for example, you selected "It curbs my appetite" as the reason for overindulging in sweets, then a potential *modifier* might be "I am as full as I healthfully need to be." Some examples will help clarify this part of Step 3. The *modifier* in each example listed below is in parentheses and italics.

a) I get angry when ignored because I feel unimportant. (*I am always important.*)

b) I don't feel good because I am overweight. (*I have a sleek physique.*)

c) I hate this work because my job is boring. (*This work excites me.*)

d) I am uncomfortable because my lower back is tense. (*My back is relaxed and loose.*)

e) Thoughts of mother irritate me. She is always critical. (*My mother cares about me.*)

Yes, you are correct, another definition for a *modifier* could be 'an untrue statement'...but only for a short while! Stay with the process, and test a potential *modifier* by assessing whether the problem would disappear if one could actually make the modifier come true. If it would you know you have arrived at an appropriate *modifier*. **Understand that the whole purpose of the Phoenix Solution is to make the *modifier* come true.** It is important to take the time necessary to arrive at a good one. (For more information on Step 3A, read Technical Manual, page 171.)

Seven Guidelines for Great Modifiers

Most changes in life are usually brought about by the inefficient trial and error method. It is smart to narrow the number of error trials by utilizing one's intelligence to select and sharpen the most appropriate *modifier*. But by what measuring stick does one determine a good *modifier*? Seven guidelines with which one can test potential *modifiers* are:

significance	_____	insignificance
clarity	_____	unclarity
complete	_____	incompleteness
specificity	_____	vaguity
precision	_____	imprecision
now-oriented	_____	future-oriented
personal	_____	impersonal

Significance vs. Insignificance

How important is it? Is this really an issue worthy of the time and energy it will take to modify it? Is this a priority item in my life?

Clarity vs. Unclarity

Am I clear on what it is I wish to modify? Am I taking the necessary time to reflect on the situation so that the real issue surfaces?

Complete vs. Incompleteness

Have I included all parts of the issue needing modification? Have I considered possible outcomes for myself and others if this modification is implemented?

Specificity vs. Vaguity

Is my assessment of the desired modification too generally stated to be useful? Do I need to be more definitive about what I want to modify?

Precision vs. Imprecision

Is my modifier fine-tuned and exact? Does it sit right with me? Is it exactly what I need?

Now-oriented vs. Future-oriented

Is my modifier stated in the present tense, which is the only place I have power? Is the modifier stated *as if* the transition had already happened, since my mind can only operate in the current moment?

Personal vs. Impersonal

Is my modifier personalized to me, using either the pronoun "I" or my name? Am I remembering that I alone have the right and power to change me?

It is important to remember that all *modifiers* may temporarily create uncomfortable feelings. This is because solving a problem is *change*, and change generally involves moving outside one's comfort zone.

Step 3. B) Shaping the modifier into a Primary Domino Thought (PDT)

The shaping of the *modifier* to its maximum effectiveness is similar to sharpening a tool for maximum efficiency. This is a critical process. The *primary domino thought* is truly the front line transformer in the Phoenix Solution. It is the workhorse, the change agent in action, the catalyst, and the magician, that will manifest the shift in your problem.

"Shaping" means shortening the *modifier* into images, numbers, or into a memorable linguistic form such as a catchy or easily remembered phrase. A sampling of some examples of linguistic primary domino thoughts includes:

"sleek physique" if one is attempting to lose weight
"make merry" if one wants to uplift one's mood
"unlock block" to unleash creativity
"finesse stress" for making peace with tension
"soothing youthing" to reduce aging

There is virtually no limit on the number of potential *primary domino thoughts* or to the areas that they might influence. They can be utilized for the narrowest of purposes, such as a headache or a thought pattern that one wishes to change, or more far-reaching and holistic lifestyle concerns, such as one's spiritual or financial development.

The best way to learn how to create *primary domino thoughts* is to just play with them. Let yourself be creative and have some fun. When one has located an effective *primary domino thought* one can easily tell by the "aha!" reaction one feels inside. The *primary domino thoughts* will click in automatically once you get the hang of it.

Step 3. C) Attach a timer, if relevant

Some *primary domino thoughts* need a time frame. Example: If one desired to lose weight, one would want the subconscious mind to terminate the command at a predetermined ideal weight such as 125 pounds, otherwise one would keep losing weight beyond the point of desirability. The fully stated *primary domino thought* with *timer* might then be "SLEEK PHYSIQUE-125 LBS."

Example: If while in a 10K race you need extra energy, the command might be issued toward the end of the race. The fully stated *primary domino thought* with *timer* inserted at the beginning of the last kilometer might be **"Emergency Energy - 'Til The Tape."**

Phoenix Solution/Step 3 - Real Examples

Terry Doubleton: Terry realizes that the reason his driving game suffers when he is upset is because he registers his frustration in his body around his neck and shoulders. This causes his swing to be too high and he ends up "skulling" the ball. Then, to compensate for that, he is dipping his right shoulder which totally throws off his swing. The *modifier* Terry derives to solve his problem on his tense days is to "relax his neck and shoulders" and he represents this with a *primary domino thought* of **"smooth, slow and easy."**

William Foxworthy: Bill is now ready to busy himself with converting one of his explanations (lack of exercise) for his problem into a goal or *modifier*, i.e., what is to be accomplished through the walking exercise program? Bill performs CCB as he dialogues with himself over the question: "How do I really want to come out of this experience?" He eventually deduces what he truly prefers in this instance is to be: a) slimmer, and b) to possess more vitality, so his *modifier* becomes "*slimmer and more energy.*" From there, and while still performing CCB, Bill sharpens the *modifier* into a *primary domino thought* which he determines to be a visualization of the amalgamated word "*Slenergy.*" Dialoguing with his doctor about his intentions, it is determined that for Bill's age and build he should optimally weigh 175 pounds, so Bill sets his *timer* at "*175 lbs*", 28 pounds below what he currently weighs. So, Bill's total *primary domino thought* with *timer* is: "*Slenergy-175 lbs.*" Bill is still highly doubtful that this will work for him.

Susan Purnell: Susan, while performing CCB, determines that her *modifier* is to "*get a solid night's sleep*" and she quickly converts this into a visualized acronym *primary domino thought* of "*SNS".* Susan sets her *timer* with a visualization of the digital numbers representing the time the alarm is to go off in the morning, "*7:30.*" Susan's total *primary domino thought* with *timer* then is "*SNS-7:30.*"

Gwendolyn Smith-Burnett: Gwen is angry. She loves dairy products and, even more, she loves many of the things that contain dairy product ingredients such as milk chocolate, cookies, bread, pastry, ice cream, etc. While breathing consciously and connectedly (CCB) into her anger she decides to alter her desire for dairy products with a *modifier* of "moving away from dairy," which in her mind suddenly and humorously converts into "mooing away" from dairy. The humor gives her the ability to loosen up and realize that this is merely a dietary paradigm shift that will open up totally new territories of adventures in eating. She decides on a *primary domino thought* as a visualization of a snapshot of herself robust, healthy and laughing. She sets no *timer*. Gwen's *primary domino thought* is a mental snapshot.

David Birnbaum: While performing CCB David quickly determines a *modifier* of "stitchless side" and converts that into the visualized *primary domino thought* of a tube for transporting conscious connected breathing (CCB) from his throat directly to the discomfort in his side, actively soothing that area with each inhale and withdrawing the tension with each exhale. No *timer* is set. David's *primary domino thought* is an animated visualization.

Elizabeth Rohrbach: While performing CCB Beth looks at her internal menu of mood choices and selects "serene" as her *modifier*. She sharpens the *modifier* into a *primary domino thought* visualization of smoothly flowing unrippled waters with her face reflected in the stream bearing a slight smile on her countenance. She sets the *timer* at "?", her symbol for "whenever." Elizabeth's *primary domino thought* is an animated visualization.

Christina Ishtar: Focusing on what makes her unhappy about overweight, Christina discovers that it is feeling clumsy, like an elephant in too small of a space. She also discovers she does not like the idea of losing anything, even weight. Rejecting the idea of losing for winning, she hits on the word "Light," which carries many positive connotations for her. She visualizes herself transforming from an elephant into an elegant woman---from heavy to light. Her *primary domino thought* becomes the word, "Eleglight." She sets her timer at 125, medically considered the correct weight for her height.

You:

A) Convert your Step 2 problem explanation into a *modifier*.

B) Test the *modifier* against the Seven Guidelines for Modifiers on page 91.

C) Shape the *modifier* into a *primary domino thought*.

_____
_____

D) Attach a *timer* if necessary.

_____

CHAPTER 10

THE PHOENIX SOLUTION - STEP 4
Implementation
Essential Step 4 Glossary
Creating the Good Moment
Shifting Contexts
Humor
Pleasant Memories
Visualization of Primary Domino Thought Implantation
Generating the Emotion of Accomplishment
Generating the Physical Sensations of Accomplishment
Two Truths You Can Believe In
Real Examples

CREATING THE PHOENIX

"A problem is a solution trying to happen."

All previous explanations and preparations bring us to the moment of truth: Implementation. For you to be successful with the Phoenix Solution, Step 4 must be instituted wholistically, involving your total being. Developing competence with Step 4 will put you in the commander's seat of converting problems into golden opportunities in your life.

Because Step 4 is the most critical of the steps, as well as the most challenging, it is important to carefully define our essential vocabulary. Please take your time and internalize the following terms and their meanings before moving to actual implementation. You don't have to memorize them, just understand them. This will maximize your benefits and minimize the number of trials it takes to do so.

Step 4 Glossary

Visualization = an internal picturing that is meaningful to you

There is no right or wrong way to visualize. The Phoenix Solution depends on your natural ability to deliberately and symbolically represent situations internally. Some clients have utilized pictures (snapshots), words or their acronyms (like a typewriter/word processor in action), cartoons/caricatures, symbols, abstractions of color and movement, or film clips (animation). Whatever form of visualization is utilized, it is the actual representative of the *primary domino thought*. It is *the* means of conveying a message to your subconscious system, which then actually carries out the transformation desired by automatically setting up the rest of the dominoes.

****

Timeline = you experiencing life

There are two 'types' of time. *Linear time* is your past-present-future in an apparent line. *Momentary time* is your consciousness operating in the present moment, which is the only time in which it *can* operate. From the latter perspective there really is no such thing as the past or the future, there are only successive moments of NOW, i.e., *momentary time*. Of course, there were moments of NOW called the *past* and there will be moments of NOW called the *future*, but your power rests solely in this moment represented by your conscious choice-making. You cannot make choices in the past or in the future. You can only make choices in the moment. Yes, you can make choices about how you will regard the past or the future, and these can be powerful choices indeed, but even then, those choices can only be made in the present moment. In other words, I can say, "You know, I guess it wasn't so bad getting fired that time when I was 25. It made me really look at where my life was heading." But I make that choice to regard that unpleasant past situation in a more pleasant light in the NOW. The same with forecasting: I can say to myself, "I can choose to see the future as scary or as exciting. I think I'll see it as exciting." But I make that choice about the future in the NOW.

TRUTH:
The more you can live in the present moment, the more power you have.

Question: When are you the least powerful? Answer: When you are unconscious. Consciousness is on a sliding scale: The further you are, in any moment, from being fully conscious the less powerful you are. Step 4 is a fully-conscious-in-the-moment process. If you are having difficulty getting into the moment, conscious connected breathing will help you get HERE AND NOW very quickly. Just two or three connected breaths will pull you into present time. But don't stop there; it is best to do CCB throughout Step 4.

Timeline representation possibilities: Let something like the visualization of a transparent hollow tube represent your linear timeline, and an opening through the top represent where you are NOW. Another option is to let the visualization of a set of railroad tracks represent your linear timeline, and a moving flatcar with you standing in the middle of it, represent your consciousness in the NOW. Or you can create your own metaphor representing the active present moment in your life.

****

Thought = awareness in the here and now; thoughts are also tools for shaping (or refraining from shaping) experience

A *thought* is in the present moment. When you boil it down there is no awareness outside of *thoughts*. Within *thought* resides your consciousness, your experience, and all of your power. Your power is represented by conscious choice-making: *Primary Domino Thoughts*. The way your life works (or doesn't) rests upon individual *thoughts*. This is wonderful, because a *thought* is the one thing you can totally control. It is this realization, plus the design of the *thought* and the manner in which you implement it, that makes all the difference in your life.

Internal representation of a thought: Let it take the form of a phrase, a set of initials (acronym) of a phrase, a picture, an animation, or a symbol.

****

Implant = a thinking inserted into the timeline

An *implant* is the deliberate insertion of a well-defined *primary domino thought* into the present moment. This is THE central tool of the Phoenix Solution. *Primary domino thought* is the noun; *implant* is the verb. You *implant* the *primary domino thought* into your consciousness which is represented by your *timeline*.

Rimplant = a replacement implant which involves an extraction of an ongoing thought

When you are aware that an *implant* is replacing a negative or inappropriate thought, an extraction must be performed at the same time as *implantation*. This is very similar to replacing a defective organ or joint in the body; the bad part goes out and the new part goes in. When a *primary domino thought* is *implanted* at the same time an *extraction* occurs, it is known as a *rimplant*.

Internal representation of an implant or rimplant: Any or all of the following utensils have proven useful as visualized methods of insertion into the visualized tube representing your *timeline* (life experience): chisel; trowel; syringe; pry bar; shovel; capsule; \ ; sliding board; etc.

****

Extraction = removal of a previously instituted implant

An *extraction* is the removal of a debilitating thought that is no longer desired, by visualizing its representation (picture, phrase, etc.) as being withdrawn. *Extraction* is the term utilized when one is only removing an old thought without inserting a new *primary domino thought*. This is done primarily when one discovers old detrimental "head tapes" that have been driving one into destructive modes of behavior. Sometimes these are negative childhood *implants* placed in us by careless or ignorant authority figures, malevolent abusers, or institutions, such as schools, religions, hospitals, etc.

Internal representation of an extraction: Visualized tools for *extraction* can be the same ones utilized in *implantation*, only in reverse. Others that have been used are *visualizations* of pipettes; grappling hooks; steam shovels; siphons; forceps; / ; bulldozers; etc.

****

Emotion-sensation = concentration of energy around an emotion with the accompanying physical sensation

Each person's physical response to emotion is unique. When you are angry, you may feel a tightening in your chest or have a queasy stomach. When you feel joy, you may feel light in weight and your chest is relaxed. It is important for you to get to know just how you individually register your emotions in your body, so you can deliberately duplicate them later.

****

[End of Glossary]

MOST IMPORTANT! Implantations are only to be implanted while you are feeling 'good.' This cannot be overemphasized.

Most humans, if they think at all to self-intervene, only do so when they are feeling badly. This is equivalent to casting seeds onto a flat rock and expecting them to grow. Your chances of success rise immeasurably if you plant the seeds in rich soil where they can take root, correct? The primary domino thought is exactly like a seed, and it needs to be implanted at a moment when one feels uplifted and the soil is rich. The challenge here is that most humans don't even think to deliberately self-design when they are feeling good. This is often the major differentiation between beginners with the Phoenix Solution and the experienced "flyers." At first, beginners see the 'good moment' as a rare opportunity to indulge as long as the ride lasts (which they know won't be long); but when they get more experience the 'feeling good moment' is seen as not only a chance to gain control over the duration of the moment, but also an opening in which to *implant* and/or reinforce a number of *primary domino thoughts* to insure a future good harvest. It becomes flat out opportunism with the highest of intentions and the ultimate of harvests.

TRUTH:
If you wish to temper the metal, you must strike while the iron is hot.

ANOTHER TRUTH:
A successful person gets up in the morning looking for an opportunity—and if there isn't one, makes it.

[If you wish to get maximum benefit from the Phoenix Solution, then also make an *implantation* regarding *willingness* to not only notice these fertile moments, but also to take advantage of them when they are present.]

How to Create the 'Good Moment'

You do not have to wait for a 'good moment.' You can create it. The idea of creating a 'good moment' is closely aligned with the ultimate goal of the Phoenix Solution. In other words, if you are feeling poorly, and in that moment have a desire to do some deliberate self-design, the fertile ground can be created in several ways. Here are some popular and effective ones.

<u>Conscious Connected Breathing (CCB)</u>

You can create the good moment by performing conscious connected breathing and relaxation until you feel uplifted, and <u>then</u> the *primary domino thought* can be implanted! CCB creates a "window" or space in which you take control of the situation (this helps right away), inhale large amounts of fresh air (this helps), eliminate a lot of waste product through the exhale (this helps), send a message to the autonomic nervous system that everything is OK (this really helps!), and induce elimination of the source of most pain, which is ultimately your resistance (this helps a whole way big bunch!), and then the relaxation signifies a readiness to make a shift. And this is all within your control no matter what is going on in the outside world! It just takes *willingness* to do it.

Shifting contexts

Another method of creating 'good moments' is by deliberately shifting contexts. We know how to do this, but we rarely do it regularly and deliberately. A *context* is the way in which we regard something. I can choose to see a flat tire many ways: a painful experience; a race to see how fast I can change the tire; a challenge to find and use the owner's manual; a chance to use my AAA dues; an opportunity to meet a passing motorist; a good story for later on; etc. It is totally up to me how I wish to experience this flat tire. Oh, and I can also choose to react the same way I always do by being angry at the inconvenience; after all, this tactic works so well! The point is, if I'm feeling badly, it has a lot to do with how I am choosing to view the situation that I am in, and I can change how I feel by changing how I regard the situation.

DO THIS: Sit and do CCB for 30 seconds and then reflect on a situation in your life that you could alter your view, then do so in as many ways as you can. Be creative, weird, or outlandish–just have fun with this. Humor is highly recommended. Notice how your body and emotions change with each new context. Practice doing this with daily situations for the next week and notice the dramatic results. One client, constantly annoyed by a power-tripping obnoxious boss, began to visualize him as naked every time she saw him. Think about it.

Humor

Another method of inducing a "feeling good" moment is through direct application of humor. Remember, you don't have to feel good to laugh...you can laugh in order to feel good. Some clients keep humorous books around (Calvin & Hobbes books are some of my favorites) to pull out and read on specific occasions when a shift is needed. You can also visualize other things that make you smile, such as cute puppies, a Charlie Chaplin sequence, or any humorous memory.

Pleasant Memories

When you are not having a good moment but you want to create one, do this: sit with your eyes closed and vividly remember a pleasant moment in your life. Picture the scenery, yourself in it, and remember all the details including the emotions that went with it. Do some CCB along with this for two minutes and notice what happens! You could try it right now just to see, couldn't you?

[Once the good moment is present or created move on to Step 4 of the Phoenix Solution]

****

Step 4. A) Visualize implantation (and extraction, if relevant) of the Primary Domino Thought with timer

While relaxing the body and performing conscious connected breathing, *implant* the *primary domino thought* along with the *timer* into the *timeline*, represented by the tube (or flatcar, or whatever you choose to represent your experiencing of life in the NOW). Do this by first visualizing the *primary domino thought*. If one is replacing a former thought, or *rimplant*, then the old thinking must be visualized as being extracted before the new thinking is implanted. Again, possible ways in which a thought can be represented internally include:

a) Visualizing the actual words, or their acronym, as on a computer screen
b) Visualizing an actual photograph or snapshot
c) Visualizing a cartoon-like or caricature-like pictorial
d) Visualizing an abstraction such as moving colors
e) Visualizing numerical characters
f) Visualizing a film clip, or animation

g) Utilizing a combination of any or all of the above.

It is extremely important to *visualize* the *primary domino thought* being inserted with a tool such as a chisel, shovel, trowel, syringe, etc. or entering your body with each inhale. It is helpful for this to be visualized several times during this phase, remembering to accompany the *implant* with conscious connected breathing and relaxation.

Step 4. B) Generating the emotion of accomplishment

Along with the breathing and relaxing, effectiveness is dramatically increased by actualizing (bringing up from within) the emotional counterparts that would accompany the realization of the solution to your problem (*modifier*). Just in case the previous sentence was confusing: The more total your involvement in bringing the new results into fruition, the more effective the outcome. Generating emotion is a very powerful entry into the subconscious mind. It involves avenues of communication monitored by the subconscious/autonomic nervous system. This bypasses the conscious system which has been responsible for keeping you locked into the thoughts which have created the need for this re-engineering! Some examples of generated emotion would be: a) the emotion of elation upon feeling a sudden burst of energy; b) the joyous self-confidence of being twenty-five pounds lighter; or, c) the serenity of an alleviated headache.

These actualizations of emotion-sensation should be done in tandem with the visualized *implantation* of the *primary domino thought*. In other words, Step 4 - A, B, C, should all be done at the same time.

Step 4. C) Generating the physical sensations of accomplishment

Imagine the physical sensations that would go with successful accomplishment as if it had already happened. Place yourself inside the *visualization*. Posture your body accordingly. If you are aiming for vitality, assume a posture of alertness and interest in your surroundings. If vitality is your goal, then at the time of *implantation* let your body get erect, head up, eyes bright and eager while breathing fully in an energized fashion. If becoming slimmer is a *modifier*, then imagine how your body would feel at that ideal weight. Can you feel the lightness, the relaxation in your tissues from not having to carry all that weight, the electricity in your body from being successful at something you thought would never happen? See yourself as slimmer and feel the emotions that go with it. Get into it!

A Summary Statement

The three parts of Step 4 should be performed repeatedly, reshaping them as one learns of more effective forms, until they are absorbed naturally into one's experience. There they can be savored and enjoyed. It cannot be overemphasized how valuable patience, persistence and a sense of adventure can be in the successful implementation of Step 4.

Phoenix Solution/Step 4 - Real Examples

Terry Doubleton: Terry has chosen "*smooth, slow and easy*" as his PDT or *primary domino thought*. Before going to sleep at night he spends three or four minutes implanting a visualization of himself swinging a golf club slowly, smoothly and easily. He chooses to do this for three nights in a row prior to his next golf match. At the first tee on that day as he is addressing the ball, Terry solidly implants the words "*slow, smooth and easy*" after taking three conscious connected breaths to relax himself, and promptly hits the ball straight down the fairway 25 yards further than usual! His game continues to improve the rest of the day as he constantly places himself in the right frame of mind with the Phoenix Solution.

A few weeks later, Terry notices his game falling off once more, because tension at the office is building again with his neck and shoulders taking on an extra burden. He realizes that the *PDT* is not working because he has failed to "feel good" when he implants it. He reflects upon a time when he felt totally relaxed and serene from his past, a time when he was a child and would lay under a tree beside a stream which ran through a woods near his home. He would watch the sun streaming through the leaves and the breeze rustling the branches, and he would feel peaceful and carefree. Using this image and the commensurate feelings as a *visualization*, Terry places himself in the proper frame of mind to empower his *primary domino thought* "**smooth, slow and easy**" before implanting it. This is almost like utilizing a *PDT* to implant a *PDT*, and it works well, restoring his game to his now customary 2 handicap.

William Foxworthy: Bill is reminded that for maximum effectiveness his *primary domino thought,* "**Slenergy**," should only be implanted when he is "feeling good," but he isn't. He is beginning to think this is a total waste of time, that it's just another weird new-age fad that promises results but fails to deliver. He is slipping into procrastinating thoughts, blaming modalities toward his spouse again, and is getting depressed. Bill is running up against his comfort zone. He suddenly remembers that if you want to change you must be prepared for short-term internal discomfort because of the natural laws of comfort zone inertia.

Bill also remembers that if you aren't feeling good naturally you can induce a "feel good" state temporarily by doing CCB, mentally recontextualizing the moment, reading or thinking of something funny, or recalling a pleasant memory. Deliberately, Bill remembers the time when in the school cafeteria his best friend, Al Beaupre, catapulted a cling peach section off his fork which travelled through the air, unbelievably disappearing into Buffy Barton's rather ample cleavage, causing Buffy to promptly blow a mouthful of chocolate milk all over Nancy Raleigh's new white cheerleading sweater. While chuckling to himself in the present moment and performing CCB, Bill visualizes his *timeline* tube and *implants* his *primary domino thought*, "**Slenergy**" and the *timer*, "**175**" through a dorsal opening. He *visualizes* the *primary domino thought* and *timer* beautifully coloring the water representing his life energy flowing through the tube and becoming a constant presence in his life. While continuing to perform CCB he allows himself to experience enthusiasm and vitality as if the goal is already accomplished. The *primary domino thought* is entrenched. Bill is solidly on his way to not only feeling the difference, but effortlessly experiencing himself performing his exercise program automatically with vitality. He may repeat this procedure as often as he sees fit, when he is feeling good. Bill has just taken a great step in his life: For the first time he is in control of his own self-design. It will only get better from here.

Susan Purnell: Settling into bed, and prepared to create a good night's sleep, Susan *visualizes* her *timeline* as a long clear flexible plastic tube about half full of liquid (her energy of experience). She feels excited about the prospect of getting a "solid night's sleep" and begins her Conscious Connected Breathing to elevate her mood in preparation for a *rimplantation*. Opening a trap door in the top of the *timeline* she *visualizes* a sliding board reaching to just above the rather turbulent waters of her present energy state. She then visualizes an extraction, "**TNT**" (for "tossin' n turning") sliding up and out of the *timeline* and, simultaneously, her *primary domino thought*, "**SNS**", sliding down the board and dropping into the water. She also slides a *visualization* of the digits "**7:30**" into the waters as her wake-up call. Allowing herself to relax with the

CCB, Susan *visualizes* over and over again the "**SNS-7:30**" sliding into the water, soothing the turbulence until the water is unrippled in its silent flow through the night. Susan awakes refreshed at exactly 7:30 just before the alarm goes off. Yes, just like that.

Gwendolyn Smith-Burnett: Gwen is so angry about her dietary restriction, that it takes her a while to remind herself to convert the anger into determination to follow the Phoenix Solution. She performs CCB, relaxes, remembers a wonderful trip to Mexico City and visualizes her *timeline* tube. In a dorsal slot on her *timeline* Gwen inserts a *primary domino thought* snapshot of herself appearing robust, healthy and happy. She sees the energy-waters becoming still and serene and notices a calming influence in her abdomen. Her emotions turn from anger to hopefulness and then relief as she focuses more and more on her proactive *visualizations* and *emotion-sensations* of accomplishment. Sooner or later she will find herself almost magically pursuing other activities that will benefit her health, perhaps meditation, or enjoying a new way of cooking and eating, or meeting people with similar issues and sharing support with them. It will feel natural and miraculous at the same time. Gwen is on her way.

David Birnbaum: David begins to perform CCB to the depths that he can, being initially restricted to shallow connected breaths because of the pain in his side. He *visualizes* the tube in his throat carrying fresh and soothing air to the stitch area with each inhale, and withdrawing more and more tension with each exhale. Reminding himself to relax and "own the stitch" he continues the breathing until there is a noticeable smoothing effect of the jagged feeling in his side. He is then encouraged to take in more air, allowing himself to feel the emotional and physical relief that accompanies the subsiding pain. Within a minute the stitch is dissolved and David turns his attention to other matters.

Elizabeth Rohrbach: Elizabeth utilizes the internal vehicle of a clear plastic tube that is 4 inches in diameter and has disappearing ends to symbolize her *timeline*. It has crystal blue waters flowing through it to represent her energy flow. To change her mood to one of serenity she opens a trap door in the dorsal side of the tube and pours her *primary domino thought* upon the waters of her life: A *visualization* of smoothly flowing unrippled waters with her smiling face reflected in the stream. She instantly notices a positive shift in her physical/emotional/ mental make-up away from the bad mood. The more she sharpens her *visualization* and perceives the waters becoming still and peaceful, the more she feels the effects. In about 30 seconds Elizabeth's mood is thoroughly shifted and she lets go of the process in order to move on to other activities.

Christina Ishtar: Christina loves gardening and so visualizes herself in a lovely garden. She soothes herself by lying in a shady, soft bed of moss beneath an old, strong, oak tree. In a nearby sunny meadow, she watches butterflies and lets herself feel light and elegant like a butterfly. In her garden, she sees a row of sad-looking weeds. Each weed has flowers shaped like numbers Christina determines to make the garden healthy and neat by removing the weeds. She takes a claw tool and begins to dig up the row of weeds. The first weed's flowers are shaped like "150," the next like "149," the next like "148." The very last weed in the row has flowers shaped like "126," Using her favorite garden trowel, Christina plants a row of beautiful, healthy plants whose petals form the number "125." She pats the soil carefully and lovingly, composts the row, and waters the plants from a nearby stream. She then takes the pulled weeds to her compost pile and turns them in, knowing they will be transformed into a rich energy source. She sits back and admires her elegant new plants, watching the butterflies skim lightly across their glowing petals. She focuses on the delight of creating her mental garden just the way she wants it: elephant free.

You:

A) Create a visualization of your *primary domino thought.*
B) Create the good moment through CCB, shifting contexts, humor, or a pleasant memory.
C) *Implant* the *primary domino thought.*
D) Feel the emotions of accomplishment.
E) Feel the physical sensations of accomplishment.

CHAPTER 11

THE PHOENIX SOLUTION - Step 5
Refinement
The Step 5 Checklist
A Note About Results
Real Examples

DOING IT BETTER

"Fine tuning makes the difference."

Refinement: The 5th Step is not always necessary. The more experience you have with the Phoenix Solution the less you will need it. This may or may not be long in coming. For now, know that if you don't get the results you want, then the 5th Step is critical to refining your application of the process until you are totally satisfied. Continue to repeat and refine Steps 1 - 4 until you acquire precision and effectiveness with the Phoenix Solution.

Step 5 completes the essential loop of feedback and refinement between goals and outcomes. It provides a space to reflect upon what you hoped would happen and what actually did happen. It provides an opportunity to continue and/or modify the pursuit of your purpose. You are strongly encouraged to "journal your journey" with the Phoenix Solution—especially with the next process.

The Step 5 Checklist

    A. What was the change desired?
    B. What *modifier* was selected to bring about the change?
    C. What *primary domino thought* was utilized?
    D. Was a *timer* indicated?
    E. Was *implantation* carried out with *visualization*?
    F. Was *implantation* carried out with the emotion of accomplishment?

G. Was *implantation* carried out with the physical sensations of accomplishment?
H. What unforeseen benefits occurred outside my purpose?
I. What unforeseen challenges occurred outside my purpose?
J. Were there additional areas or objectives uncovered during the process?
K. Were my results satisfactory?
L. If not, should A - E be modified and in what manner?
M. Do the 5-steps again.

It is indeed possible for a single application of a *primary domino thought* to create the long-term results you desire. Excellent results in just one application frequently happen, and there is absolutely no good reason why they shouldn't happen every time. There are plenty of not-so-good reasons, however, and in these cases it will take a persistent and patient effort at repeating and refining the *modifier* and the derived *primary domino thought* until success is achieved. You will learn from these adjustments. You will learn how to be efficient and effective in applying the Phoenix Solution. By working through Steps 1 - 4 you will always arrive at the correct destination. Your accuracy in appraisal and application increases with persistent *awareness* and *willingness*. Be willing to take action again and again, if necessary. Never give up.

A Note About Results

That the Phoenix Solution works is irrefutable because there are so many success stories, but exactly *how* the results exhibit themselves is variable, not only from person to person, but from application to application within a person. It is good advice to let go of the need to arm wrestle the results from the process (as 'science' erroneously attempts to do) and concentrate on the process.

DO THIS: Ride easy in the saddle with controlling results; just persistently do your best and leave the rest.

Results with the Phoenix Solution run the continuum from *instant* all the way to *gradual*. Mood changes can occur in an eyeblink. Have you ever experienced "insight," or suddenly had a "change of heart"? Have you ever been in one mood, heard a song on the radio, and then been suddenly transported into another mood? You now can make these shifts deliberately by internalizing the Phoenix Solution, and using it whenever you prefer another mood. Body sensations can be altered the same way. You have experienced, no doubt, the sudden onset or cessation of an itch, twitch, tension, or any muscular movement. The sensation is suddenly there and then, just as suddenly, it is not. You can now deliberately create and delete physical sensations. Thoughts are suddenly there, and then they are not. You can choose this outcome as well. A little practice and persistence and you can master all of these functions at will. By mastering mood, sensation and thought, you master the world.

Some areas of behavioral change will perhaps take longer because you have identified the wrong cause and, therefore, need to heed Step 5 rigorously. *Lack of results is a major clue.* The process cannot be "wrong" for you - it can only be applied correctly and effectively or incorrectly and less effectively. Some areas of behavior will take longer because they are complex, and you will discover all the "subparts" that need addressing as you go. Don't be disheartened - see it as an adventure. You are safe and you are doubtlessly going to wind up in a better place, even if you cannot always predict exactly where. So, you may think the problem of thirty pounds you have put on is why your spouse has lost interest in your sex life, and you utilize the Phoenix Solution to lose the 30 pounds, only to find out that it wasn't the weight, but something else that needs addressing. So what has happened here? A) You lost 30 pounds; B) You found out you *can do that* on your own; C) You have more confidence in yourself (overcoming 30 pounds is a very tangible confidence builder!); D) You are more adept at utilizing the Phoenix Solution (overcoming 30 pounds is a very tangible skills builder!); and, very importantly, E) You may now correctly identify the problem and have a proven vehicle with which to do something about it! The journey is successful. Although the exact outcome was never predicted by you in the beginning, without the beginning there would have been no successful outcome!

Sometimes results are highly visible only in retrospect. Often at the Institute for Transformational Studies we receive calls from amazed people saying, "I just noticed that : a) I don't have the urge to smoke/drink/etc. anymore; b) I don't have those crazy feelings anymore; c) I don't have those obsessive thoughts anymore about insecurity/work/my children/money/etc.; or, d) My lower backaches have been gone for three days/my body is healing so rapidly [in various ways]/my headaches are gone/etc." These delayed results are a thrill, much like unexpectedly receiving a holiday gift in the mail a week late. They are also a tribute to the true power of a single thought when thoughtfully applied.

Phoenix Solution/Step 5 - Real Examples

Despite success with the Phoenix Solution, Terry & Bill & Sue & Gwen & David & Beth & Christina will forget to use it many, many times when it could benefit them. It is with time and practice that they will A) notice the situations where the Phoenix Solution can work for them; and, B) apply the Phoenix Solution more and more efficiently, effectively and quickly. What will be the rest of the story for **You**?

Sometimes it will be memory that reminds one of the Phoenix Solution's useful existence. Sometimes it will be emotional pain that causes remembrance of the relief available. Often a sense of energizing empowerment will arrive through consciousness of a single breath. The awareness of that single breath creates the window of opportunity, the moment rich with power for creating your happiness.

CHAPTER 12

CONCLUSION
The Phoenix Solution Outline
Designing Your World

THE PHOENIX SOLUTION

Outline

The Five Steps

STEP 1: TRANSFORMING PROBLEMS INTO PASSION
"To change anything, you must first get close."

___Have you passionately possessed the problem by being willing to accept it as your experience alone?
___Are you mentally ready to take full responsibility for solving this problem?
___Are you doing Conscious Connected Breathing so that your body is exhibiting acceptance of the problem?

STEP 2: DEVELOPING THE PROBLEM
"Learn the exact nature of the problem, and who owns it."

___Have you thoroughly considered the possible causes of your problem?
___From all the possible causes have you selected the one that feels most correct?
___Have you stated the most accurate explanation for your problem?
___Are you positive that the problem is yours and yours alone?
___Is the problem clearly and succinctly stated?

STEP 3: PRODUCING THE PRIMARY DOMINO
"Generate the magic formula."

___Have you converted your problem statement into its positive mirror image, or *modifier*?
___Does your modifier meet these guidelines?
  a) It is significant to me.
  b) It is clear to me.
  c) It seems complete to me.
  d) It is specific.
  e) It is precise.
  f) It is stated in the present tense.
  g) It is personally stated (the pronoun "I" is used, if any).
___Have you shaped the *modifier* statement into a *primary domino thought* representative symbol, phrase, graphic, etc.?
___If necessary, have you attached a *timer*?

STEP 4: CREATING THE PHOENIX
"A problem is a solution trying to happen."

___Have you created the good moment by doing CCB, shifting contexts, using humor, or remembering something pleasant?
___Did you visualize the implantation/rimplantation of your *primary domino thought* and *timer*?
___Did you generate the emotion of accomplishment?
___Did you generate the physical sensations of accomplishment?

STEP 5: DOING IT BETTER
"Fine tuning makes the difference."

___Use the Step 5 Checklist (pg. 115) to refine your procedure.
___A. What was the change desired?
___B. What *modifier* was selected to bring about the change?

___C. What *primary domino thought* was utilized?
___D. Was a *timer* indicated?
___E. Was *implantation* carried out with *visualization*?
___F. Was *implantation* carried out with the emotion of accomplishment?
___G. Was *implantation* carried out with the physical sensations of accomplishment?
___H. What unforeseen benefits occurred outside my purpose?
___I. What unforeseen challenges occurred outside my purpose?
___J. Were there additional areas or objectives uncovered during the process?
___K. Were results satisfactory?
___L. If not, in what manner should A - E be modified?
___M. Do the 5-steps again.

Conclusion to the User's Manual

Designing Your World

Psychotechnology, and the empowerment it represents, marks the dawning of a significant paradigm shift in human existence. It may someday be noted as the beginning of the end of human suffering as we know it, and the birth of a healthy, caring, and thriving global society. It will start with people just like you, deciding to design and implement elegant thinking on a deliberate basis. It can potentially spread like a benevolent wave across this world of ours because of people just like you, consciously and conscientiously applying *primary domino thoughts* to create health, wealth, and happiness.

Part Two

TECHNICAL MANUAL

APPENDIX I

THE MAP OF MODIFICATION (MOM)

&

The Phoenix Solution Ancillary

INTRODUCTION

It is interesting to note that this section was added to the *Phoenix Flight Manual* long after Part I was successfully field-tested in three versions. The first version, which I now personally view as awkward, confusing and incomplete, helped people create great results in their lives! Literally hundreds of people have availed themselves of Psychotechnology in Part I of this volume without ever seeing the information you have available to you now. Part I is the real "doing" part of the Manual.

Part II is explanatory and, like most Technical Manuals, only a linguistic resemblance of the actual experience. Please remember that the value and the gift of the *Phoenix Flight Manual* is in the Doing. If you spend a solid month practicing the contents of the Manual to get it down pat, it would be the best dedicated study you ever performed. After all, what is more important than being able to manifest health and happiness at will?

The Technical Manual offers in-depth coverage of some Part I topics, and a few other helpful items that belong in an Appendix. If you are like me, sometimes you like to dig a little deeper into things you are interested in, looking for little kernels of information that can spark a new direction, perhaps even a new Primary Domino Thought that could change your life.

THE MAP OF MODIFICATION (MOM)

Issues and Focus Areas in The Matter of Change

The attempt is to carefully define the time lapse stages in the matter of making a change in one's life. The need for change could be from discovering that you are sitting on something that is uncomfortable, to stopping smoking, readjusting your disposition, eliminating disease, fixing a relationship, losing weight, changing churches, altering your golf swing, or correcting a child. With the help of such a map one can find where one is bogged down, and gain assistance in clearing away the obstacles to successful change. The field of Psychotechnology, as represented by the Phoenix Solution in this manual, facilitates the most complex stages of 4 - 10. The chart begins at the bottom, progressing upwards, to return homeostatically to Contentment. Each step births the next step, thus another reason for the "MOM" acronym.

The Map of Modification
[Begin at the bottom]

[Repeat the stages]
^
CONTENTMENT IS RE-ESTABLISHED
^
10. FINE TUNING IS PERFORMED
^
9. THE MODIFIER IS APPLIED
^
8. A SPECIFIC MODIFIER IS DEVELOPED
^
7. A CONSCIOUS COMMITMENT TO TAKE ACTION IS PRESENT
^
6. THE PROBLEM IS CLEARLY DEVELOPED
^
5. THE PROBLEM IS PASSIONATELY POSSESSED
^
4. AN INTERNAL LOCUS OF CONTROL IS ESTABLISHED
^
3. THE GENERAL AREA NEEDING ADJUSTMENT IS LOCATED
^
2. AN UNCONSCIOUS INTENTION TO CHANGE THE SITUATION IS REGISTERED
^
1. AN AWARENESS OF DISCOMFORT AND/OR DESIRE ARISES
^
CONTENTMENT EXISTS

Phoenix Flight Manual 131

The map is utilized by selecting an unsolved problem, tracking it upwards until reaching a stage that one has been unable to complete, then beginning exploration towards solving that stage so that one can move closer to the end of the modification process. After performing all stages, one achieves completion of that particular modification problem with an end result resembling a successful ratchet effect. If one "breaks down" at any of the stages one has to start over (much like a broken ratchet that doesn't catch) until one is able to complete that particular stage. A "chronic problem" is being stuck in the pipeline at the same place over and over again, which is why we become so inflamed when we begin feeling that "Here it comes again!" feeling.

Many believe that motivation to change things is brought about through *pushing*. Abraham Maslow, the godfather of motivation theory, has clearly shown in *The Farther Reaches of Human Nature* that more effective and permanent change is created by clearing away obstacles or lower levels of needs so that one is *pulled* upwards. This is based on the belief, substantiated by an extensive body of research, that human beings are equipped and, therefore, destined to develop. I prefer *rising* to the top rather than being *kicked* to the top. Frederick Herzberg, the great grandpa of industrial psychology, spoke of negative and positive KITAs (Kicks In The Ass). Even with his favoritism towards executive/owners rather than the workers, he still stated there was really no difference between being kicked in the butt or having a carrot dangled in front of your nose. One was more positive and preferable, but still a KITA.

It is important for the reader to understand the quantum difference between just getting temporarily positive KITAs out of life and utilizing the Map of Modification to move permanently and progressively forward in life. The MOM was developed to help clarify the obstacles that need clearing away so that one's finest human attributes can naturally *rise* to the surface. It is based on a positive view of the pristine spiritual human being. When a human is functioning healthfully, its natural state is one of wonderful, enhancing and enthusiastic performance. When humans operate dysfunctionally they are neglectful, and inwardly and outwardly abusive. Removing obstacles converts dysfunctionality into functionality and allows the true human spirit to thrive and benefit all that it contacts. Psychotechnology is all about liberating people and the planet from incapacitation and limitation, i.e., eliminating pain and confusion.

Contentment

It behooves us to define just what we mean by *contentment*. I define contentment as that which we are satisfied with, i.e. that which we do not wish to change further. For some this is serenity or peacefulness, and for others it might be a state of adventure, or even precariousness. In others it might even be a state of discomfort, such as St. Francis of Assisi who only felt content when he was suffering, or ourselves when we have done something wrong and only feel content if we feel guilty (penance). It is true that our concept of contentment for ourselves varies; sometimes we want just peace and quiet, and other times we need something akin to a rollercoaster effect to feel content with the moment. Suffice it to say that contentment is whatever state you wish to be in, whether it is one you wish to return to (discomfort-based motivation) or one you wish to attain in the future (desire-based motivation).

We may also speak of momentary contentment versus "a contented life," or a life with fullness and meaning. Two major questions we can ask ourselves include: "What is the meaning of life?" and "What is my mission, vision, and purpose in this life?" Psychotechnology is designed to assist with achieving both momentary and mission types of contentment. For our explanatory purposes here we will look at momentary contentment. (A mission development process is located in Appendix III. One way of viewing mission fulfillment is as a series of momentary contentment maps.)

To get on with it, let us just agree that our constant momentary objective is to direct our energies (thoughts, words and deeds) towards "feeling good" in some way, and that feeling good is another way of being in a state of contentment. As long as we are content we have no need to modify, but when a discomfort or a desire raises its head we are kicked out of a state of contentment and thrust into a mode of seeking modification. We might even go so far as to say that all motivation, including motivation towards progress, is created by a state of discontent.

This is where the Map of Modification (MOM) can be of assistance as a means of diagnosing exactly where we are stuck in our drive to achieve contentment. The MOM can be utilized by self-helping individuals and modification professionals (service occupations such as teachers, counselors, therapists, social workers, medical personnel, ministers, etc.) as a diagnostic tool to remove blockages to recovery and/or development. The MOM illustrates the pathway of self-initiated change no matter what means of modification are eventually utilized. The Phoenix Solution is one psychotechnological means of accelerating the accomplishment of the MOM, stages 4 - 10.

In order to get a clear picture of the MOM in action let us take a simple sample problem and work through it in slow motion.

I'm sitting at the computer working on this manuscript and I'm enjoying doing it (CONTENTMENT EXISTS). I notice an ache. (1. AN AWARENESS OF DISCOMFORT AND/OR DESIRE ARISES). I don't like aches, so I want to remove it (2. AN INTENTION TO CHANGE THE SITUATION IS REGISTERED). I narrow the area of the ache to inside me, my lower back (3. THE GENERAL AREA NEEDING ADJUSTMENT IS LOCATED). I decide that I am responsible for fixing the situation (4. AN INTERNAL LOCUS OF CONTROL IS ESTABLISHED). I feel very strongly about doing something about the situation (5.THE PROBLEM IS PASSIONATELY POSSESSED). Upon examination, I realize that I am sitting forward on the edge of the chair, slumping forward instead of taking advantage of this $160 chair's specially designed lower back support feature (6. THE PROBLEM IS FULLY DEVELOPED). I quickly determine that I am the best candidate to make the modification needed (7. A COMMITMENT TO TAKE ACTION IS PRESENT). I decide the best solution is to slide my posterior backwards into the structure designed to support it (8. A SPECIFIC MODIFIER IS DEVELOPED). I move my rear rearwards (9. THE MODIFIER IS APPLIED). I wiggle around until it is just right (FINE TUNING IS PERFORMED). I return my focus to my writing (CONTENTMENT IS RE-ESTABLISHED).

Let's take a more complex issue and see how it might run smoothly. After this we will take the same issue and show potential trouble areas and issues that can occur when things do not go smoothly. We will use that framework to thoroughly detail the Map of Modification and, therefore, its value as a diagnostic tool when things go awry. Utilizing a relationship issue as an exploratory paradigm of stereotypical perfection with the MOM, we shall look in on Bill and Jill. (Remember, this is just a simple scenario to idealistically portray the stages of the Map of Modification. This scenario incorporates the steps of the Phoenix Solution, but not the technology.)

Bill and Jill have been married for a year and things are going very well (CONTENTMENT EXISTS). Then one day Jill notices Bill is staying later and later at the office when, previously, he couldn't wait to get home to see her (DISCOMFORT ARISES). At first Jill excuses it, but when it appears to be a pattern, it becomes too uncomfortable to ignore (AN UNCONSCIOUS INTENTION TO CHANGE THE SITUATION IS REGISTERED). Communication involving both parties seems to be in order (THE GENERAL AREA NEEDING ADJUSTMENT IS LOCATED). Jill feels it is within her power to do something about this problem

(AN INTERNAL LOCUS OF CONTROL IS ESTABLISHED). Since Bill does not appear upset at coming home later, Jill realizes that she is the one in discomfort, therefore it is her problem (THE PROBLEM IS PASSIONATELY POSSESSED). Upon investigation, Jill discovers that Bill is trying to get a promotion, so he is staying late to put in some voluntary overtime to make a good impression (THE PROBLEM IS CLEARLY DEVELOPED). For additional reassurance, Jill decides to request some affirmation of the value of the marriage to Bill (A COMMITMENT TO TAKE ACTION IS PRESENT). Jill formulates a question (A SPECIFIC MODIFIER IS DEVELOPED). Jill lets Bill know how she feels, and asks if he misses her as much as she misses him in the evenings (THE MODIFIER IS APPLIED). Bill reassures Jill that he does and will return to his usual arrival time as soon as the project he is working on is completed. Jill feels better and decides to busy herself with a work project of her own every evening while awaiting Bill's temporary delayed arrival from work (FINE TUNING IS PERFORMED). Jill is reassured, feels complete about the issue, and enjoys her new project (CONTENTMENT IS RE-ESTABLISHED).

Having just witnessed how things can run well, let's ruin the whole scenario by getting a little more realistic. We will utilize Bill and Jill's hard luck twins, Randy and Candy, as volunteers in showing just how rough it can get when the Map of Modification is not followed well. We will also use this opportunity to examine each of the first four stage's underlying ramifications.

Since they met at happy hour after work on a Friday evening, things have been going well in Randy and Candy's six month relationship (CONTENTMENT).

1. AN AWARENESS OF DISCOMFORT AND/OR DESIRE ARISES

Randy notices that the only time Candy seems happy is when they are drinking alcohol and then only after two or three drinks.

Actually this pattern of mood altering with alcohol has been going on since the first night Randy and Candy met, but Randy just now "let himself" become aware of it. It could be that Randy has been in denial about Candy's need to use chemicals in order to feel normal, or maybe he is ignorant. Perhaps he came out of a family that never drank, so he has never been exposed to such behavior, and just figures he is naive. Perhaps he doesn't want to see the truth, because it would upset the fun time they have been having, meaning that he maintains an illusion that everything is fine so that he doesn't have to realize that he has already moved out of a state of contentment. One way that people avoid confrontation is to avert their gaze—literally or figuratively.

Some clear definition of terms or areas of concern regarding awareness or lack thereof is helpful.

Avoidance: Consciously looking the other way.
Confrontation: Telling the truth.
Delusion: Believing a lie to be a truth.
Denial: An unconscious blindness regarding the truth.
Dissociation: Separating from the self in order to avoid the painful truth. Dissociative states range from ordinary daydreams, to habitual trances, to the extreme of multiple personality disorders.
Illusion: Wishfully believing in a fantasy.

Insane: Repeating the same behaviors and expecting different results.
Naive: Lacking in knowledge and/or experience. Ignorance can only be bliss in a state of momentary contentment. Ignorance is never wholistically blissful in the long run.
Stupid: Apparently unable to learn.

A metaphor for awareness is in how various people might regard their car's dashboard. Some are just naive because they haven't read the owner's manual. Some are dissociated from its importance, and fail to see what it has to do with driving. Some people are just stupid or insane, and keep running out of oil or gas repeatedly without noticing the warnings. Some might believe the illusion that if it is Allah's will they will constantly have a full gas tank without having to do anything. Some believe that by not looking at the gauge they will not run out of gas (a combination of avoidance and illusion). Someone else may truly believe the gas gauge is broken when it isn't and, therefore, ignores it (delusion). And someone else might just accept the truth that when the gauges confront them with a warning, they mean it. Then there's Jim Bob, who is in denial: he spray paints his dashboard because the truth makes him nervous.

Many do not believe that the truth will set you free, and, consequently become stuck in the first stage of the MOM. It is perhaps unfortunate that this lesson has to be learned by some of us in such painful ways, and maybe sometimes that must be the way, but humans are not cut out to favorably navigate life unconsciously. As Ellen Langer stated so well in *Mindfulness*, "Mindlessness limits our control by preventing us from making intelligent choices." Basically we wind up shackled by our own lack of awareness. Needless to say, few of us like being imprisoned. Psychotechnology is ultimately about liberation, and the first step of liberation is awareness.

"*In order to escape from prison the first thing you must know is that you are in one.*"

...William Blake

2. AN UNCONSCIOUS INTENTION TO CHANGE THE SITUATION IS REGISTERED.

Randy fails to register that anything can be done about the situation, despite being uncomfortable and playing second fiddle to alcohol. [Remember, we are doing worst case scenarios here.]

Randy thus allows the predicament to continue because his brain is conditioned to ignore certain choices that might be productive for him. It is at this level that one activates the system that carves up all the potential realities into available-to-me/unavailable-to-me categories before we are aware that this is being done. The group of cells in the brain which monitors sensory messages is known as the *reticular activating system*. It is a natural filtering device that allows only personally profitable data or threats to get through to our conscious mind. It is that part of our brain which can account for such activities as a sleeping mother hearing her baby cry, although it's cry is not as loud as the rumbling garbage truck or overhead passenger jet which did not awaken her. The reticular activating system is a mechanism intended to help focus our attention.

The second stage of the MOM is about waking the giant within (that part of the mind which you have chosen to remain unaware of known as the *unconscious*), so that you can have all potential resources at your command, as opposed to a mere narrow slice of them. Some practices that will place you in touch with your unconscious are: meditation; reflection; reading material on consciousness expansion; conscious connected breathing; Vivation; Holotropic Breathwork; Hakomi therapy; hypnosis; deep tissue massage; an open and accepting attitude; or willingness plus patience.

3. THE GENERAL AREA NEEDING ADJUSTMENT IS LOCATED.

Randy does eventually notice that he has an intention to change the situation, but he mislocates the area needing adjustment by thinking that he is just being naive.

How old is this still pertinent joke?:

The guy is crawling on all fours under a street lamp on 5th Street.
The cop comes up and says, "What are you doing?"
The guy says, "Looking for my car keys."
The cop says, "Where did you lose them?"
The guy says, "Over on 4th Street."
The cop says, "Then why aren't you looking over there?"
The guy says, "Because the lighting is so much better here."

Within a split second after experiencing an unconscious intention to change the situation, we turn our attention toward the possible area needing adjustment in order to accomplish the object of our desire or alleviate our discomfort. Not to be confused with steps 5 and 6, step 3 is a major determinant of those steps because it is about the *direction of focus*. It is a critical decision, often made unconsciously, that thrusts you into an arena which will more than likely be the "home" of your problem until it is solved, whether it is the most efficacious direction or not. The danger inherent in this stage is that it is so embedded in unquestioned automaticity. We have a very LARGE investment in emphasizing the correctness of our judgments—even the quick ones established by our narrow and historically-based habits. The need to be right is as strong as the need to survive, or sometimes even stronger; many people have prematurely gone to their grave along with their insistence upon being right! At the very least, being erroneously convinced you are right severely limits new opportunities and experiences.

A wise determination of the "general area needing adjustment" would refuse snap judgements and check out such potential territories, as represented below. If the determination is accurate, one at least begins the game in the right ballpark. We can graphically represent this as follows:

Key:
Inner Circle = Inside Me
Outer Circle = Outside Me
* = Location of the problem (Problem = situation to be changed)

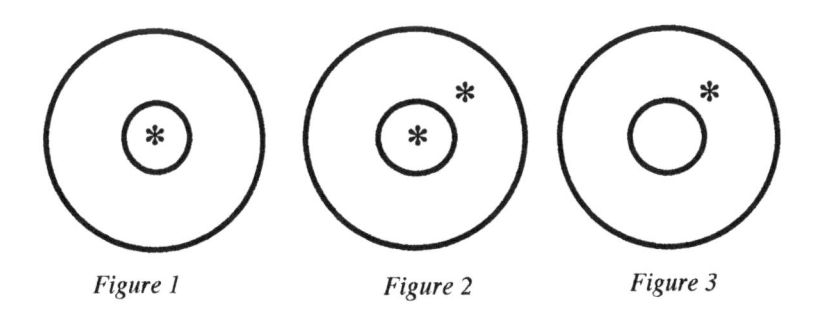

Figure 1   *Figure 2*   *Figure 3*

Figure 1) The problem is inside me.
Figure 1 represents an internal, or INDEPENDENT, orientation. Usually this is the most empowered position, as one has total ownership of the problem location.

Figure 2) The problem is both inside and outside me.
Figure 2 represents a mutual, or INTERDEPENDENT, orientation. Usually this is the second most empowered position, because one has a shared ownership in the problem location.

Figure 3) The problem is outside me.
Figure 3 represents an external, or DEPENDENT, orientation. Usually this is a fairly unempowered position, as one must rely on another person or source to make the right decision.

Unfortunately, Stage 3 often becomes automatic in most people due to their historically-based habituations. Because of this reflexive response, and because the window of awareness opens and closes so fast, it is easy to mislocate the source of the problem needing remediation. <u>It should never be taken for granted or assumed, without thoughtful reflection, where the general area needing modification is located.</u> The price for inaccurate judgment at this stage can be disastrous, and, therefore, accounts for many human-initiated disasters. Many people overlook this extremely significant stage, even mental health professionals. Humility, reflectiveness and patience are invaluable qualities in the important search for accurate diagnosis.

4. AN INTERNAL LOCUS OF CONTROL IS ESTABLISHED

Because Randy thinks the problem is his naivete' (not being "cool" enough) rather than Candy's drinking, he fails to locate the power to control the situation in Candy where it belongs. Rather than confront Candy he decides to hang out in the bar and drink more with Candy so he can learn to be less naive about the bar scene.

Stage 3 of the MOM was all about locating the general area needing adjustment, and Stage 4 is a natural next step. Now that the disturbed area is located, the question is: Where is the power to do anything about the disturbance located? This basically creates a third characteristic in this important preassessment phase. The first characteristic is the inside/outside dimension; the second characteristic is the location of the disturbance; and, the third characteristic is the location of power, or controllability. We can represent this again with our concentric circles for the inside/outside dimension, an * for the location of the disturbance, and then add shading to denote the locus of control. This provides a graphically clear means of communicating the geography of disturbances and the location of resources to deal with them. Remember, we are only talking problem and power location in this stage, yet the three possible combinations represent 9 major inculcated belief systems, or postures, towards life.

Key:
Inner Circle = Inside Me
Outer Circle = Outside Me
* = Location of the problem (or thing to be changed)
Gray = A Locus of Control
White = A Non-locus of Control

The 9 Approaches to Life

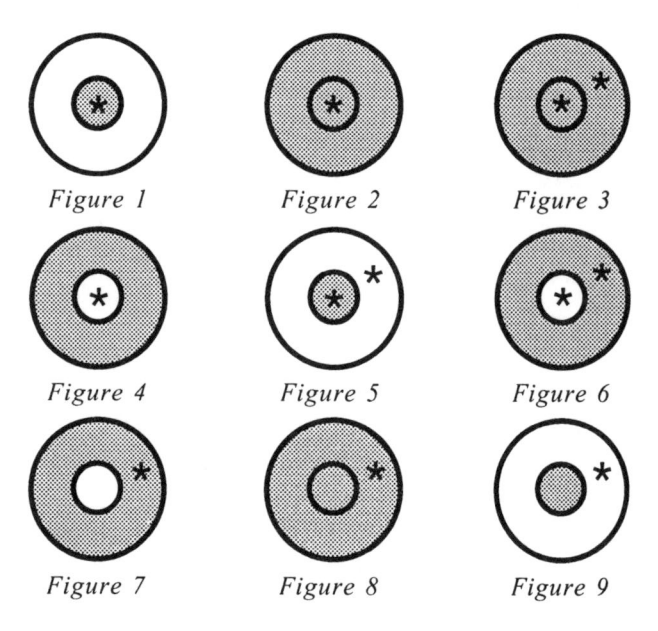

Figure 1 *Figure 2* *Figure 3*
Figure 4 *Figure 5* *Figure 6*
Figure 7 *Figure 8* *Figure 9*

Fig 1. The problem is only inside me, as is the locus of control.

Fig 2. The problem is only inside me and the locus of control is both inside and outside me.

Fig 3. The problem is both inside and outside, as is the locus of control.

Fig 4. The problem is only inside me but the locus of control is outside me.

Fig 5. The problem is both inside and outside me, but there is a locus of control inside me only.

Fig 6. The problem is both inside and outside me, but the locus of control is outside me only.

Fig 7. The problem is only outside me, as is the locus of control.

Fig 8. The problem is only outside me and the locus of control is both inside and outside me.

Fig 9. The problem is only outside me and the locus of control is inside me.

Phoenix Flight Manual 145

To expand on these a little, The 9 Approaches to Life are:

Figure 1 says the source of discomfort or desire is within me and I can do something about it–a very empowered position. "*It's my stuff and I can handle it.*"
Example: I realize I have a smoking problem and I am going to take action to stop.

Figure 2 says the source of discomfort or desire is within me and up to both me and external resources to do something about it–a potentially collaborative situation to help me out. "*It's my stuff and I can handle it with your help.*"
Example: I realize I have a smoking problem and with the help of Smokenders I can stop.

Figure 3 says the source of discomfort or desire is both inside and outside me and so are the resources to do something about it–a mutually beneficial collaborative relationship. "*It's our problem. We can fix it.*"
Example: Our relationship is hurting because of things we have both done, and we work to fix it.

Figure 4 says the source of discomfort or desire is within me and only outside resources can do anything about it–a very dependent and potentially co-dependent (compulsively destructive addiction) situation. "*It's my stuff and only you can do something about it.*"
Example: I am constantly insecure and always need reassurance from you that things will be okay.

Figure 5 says the source of discomfort or desire is both inside and outside but only I possess the resources to do something about it–a loner position. "*I am Spartacus.*"
Example: I feel uneasy living in a filthy neighborhood, and no else will clean it up so I do it by myself.

Figure 6 says the source of discomfort or desire is both inside and outside me, but only you possess the power to do anything about it. "*Please fix us.*"
Example: Our marriage is coming apart because of things we have both done or not done, so I send you to the marriage counselor.

Figure 7 says the source of discomfort or desire is only outside me, and so is the locus of control. "*It's not my fault.*"
Example: I can't help you because this is **your** problem.

Figure 8 says the source of discomfort or desire is only outside me, but the resources to fix it are both inside me and outside me. "*Through teamwork we can solve their problem.*"
Example: We work together to solve the endangered whale population.

Figure 9 says the source of discomfort or desire is only outside me, but the locus of control is inside me. "*I am the Messiah.*"
Example: You messed up the house/relationship/company/world while I was gone, but I'll clean it up for you.

Of course it is possible that there is no control for any problem no matter where it is—very helpless people who need constant managed care in order to survive.
Example: People with extremely retarded abilities and/or a situation of absolute chaos with no sense of order.

Our friend Randy should select either Figure 3 ("The problem is your drinking and my need to hang around you while you are doing it, so let's work on this together if the relationship is worth anything to you. It is to me, so how about it?") or even Figure 7 ("You have a personal drinking problem, and only you can do something about it. Please get to it."), but instead mislocates by erroneously selecting Figure 1 or Figure 4 which basically leaves him helplessly continuing in a potentially destructive relationship. In short, he winds up spending all his energy in a futile gesture to please a potential/actual alcoholic instead of making a healthy and productive decision to either take care of himself or confront Candy, her drinking, and its potential for destroying the relationship.

One of the complexities of life is finding the motivation to bring about the changes desired or needed. It gets even more complex with poor identification of the general area of the problem and the location of power to transform the problem productively. If these are done properly and accurately, one moves smoothly to the next stage. If not, one winds up dissipating energy into confusion and emotion to no avail. When nothing works, then all that's left is pain and the tempting world of compulsive behaviors that try to mask it. Remember that a problem is nothing more than a solution trying to happen. Accuracy at assessment and getting out of the way of your own progress towards solution is sometimes all that is required.

[At this point along the way of describing the Map of Modification, we begin to run a parallel course with the five steps of the Phoenix Solution. The Phoenix Solution is featured in this book as the foremost method of applied Psychotechnology, a relatively new field of endeavor which necessitates background to help establish perspective.]

A Brief History of Psychotechnology

It is interesting to note that many "innerspace pioneer seekers" arrived at similar transformational techniques without conferring or even knowing of others' work. As an example, the Phoenix Solution was developed along with the term *psychotechnology* (never having read *The Aquarian Conspiracy* by Marilyn Ferguson where it was first termed) by me prior to my reading most of the references in the Bibliography. Performing historical research for this volume found me delighted to learn of unknown colleagues of mine. I have the sneaking suspicion that we all developed our technology pretty much in isolation. This is no surprise, considering the realm of endeavor is personally independent transformation!

This independent facet of personal transformation that seems to have evolved is in itself an historical Primary Domino. As best as anyone knows, the oldest form of practical spiritual psychology originated in the time of the Ice Age as exhibited in ancient art work on cave walls in southern France. Dated about 35,000 years ago, these drawings depict *shamans* in the clans at that time conducting transformative rituals. Shamanism (pronounced either SHAH-man-izm or SHAY-man-izm from the Russian Prakrit *shamana*, "one who exhausts the life-forces in supernatural feats") became a world-wide practice over the centuries, manifesting itself in almost every culture in one form or another. No matter what the form, from wizard to medicine man to Carlos Castenada's Don Juan, they were, and still are, dedicated to intense concentration and superrevelation of the vital forces. (A significant work on shamanism is Mircea Eliade's *Shamanism: Archaic Techniques of Ecstasy*.) Throughout the world, the main features of archaic and new age shamanism remain amazingly uniform and consistent. Culturally, it is viewed as a mystical set of behaviors entered into by a select group of men and women who became consumed by spiritual powers, awakening paranormal abilities and ushering in the transformed person: One with spiritual authority and magical powers.

Psychotechnology is the 21st Century quantum mentality corollary of archaic shamanism. It seeks to tap into powers through intense concentration upon the application of specific thoughts and thought patterns in order to release the vital forces contained in their energy in an authoritative and powerful way. It does, indeed, appear to be magic (no evidence through the five senses that the effect has a cause) to the uninformed. To the practitioner of Psychotechnology, whether it be the Phoenix Solution or some other form, it makes perfect sense. It is not always Newtonian (logical/predictable), and it involves unique altered states of consciousness brought on naturally, but with a purpose towards a positive end. It is an experientially applied science in every sense of the word. Imagine the difference between reading a description of a Van Gogh versus actually seeing one up close versus creating one yourself. Imagine reading about transformation versus experiencing it. The *Phoenix Flight Manual* has no value without the experiencing of what it can do for the individual aspirant.

The roots of Psychotechnology in the New Age movement probably rest in the late 19th century with people like Phineas Quimby, an American clockmaker who converted Friederick Anton Mesmer's *mesmerism* into self-hypnosis and called it the Science of Health and Happiness. Another historical correlate was Mary Baker Eddy's Christian Science and Ernest Holmes' Science of Mind, both based on changing reality by changing the way one thinks (or doesn't think) about it. In 1906 the term *New Age* was first established by A. R. Orage, an affiliate of George Bernard

Shaw's, in his periodical dedicated to communitarianism by the same name. Orage later went on to become an ardent follower of and advocate for G. I. Gurdjieff, who around the time of WW I, was espousing a regimen of radical spiritual training to free people from their "trances," i.e., become empowered. It was in 1922, when Orage had a spiritual awakening with Gurdjieff, that the meaning of the term *New Age* itself was redefined from one of communally-based reawakening to that of individual transformation. When Orage dropped from his prestigious position as a noted writer/publisher to become a devotee of the baffling Gurdjieff, he instrumentally shifted the paradigm of what we call self-help to one of "helping the world by helping the self," from "help yourself by helping the world." (I believe that Nazism and Communism were actually the violent and convulsive death throes of the outdated sacrifice-for-society philosophy.) A harbinger of today's mode of personal seeking was also incidentally established by Orage. A man of great sequential and logical literary skills, Orage could offer no rationally adequate explanation for his transformation. He was, in effect, experiencing the relevance of modern day chaos theory, an accounting of how the world really works—not always logical, not always sequential, not always predictable, and certainly influenced in major ways by seemingly minor events. Once the Primary Domino Thought falls, things begin to happen with the speed and exact definition of the process being unpredictable. We can only be logical and mechanical up to the point where predictability and attempts to explain and contain are defied—the point known as the *quantum leap*.

Well Quimby, Eddy, Holmes, Orage, Gurdjieff, et al., set the *individual effort => change reality* paradigm into domino motion. See this as one strand of dominoes that, as monumental as it was, was still, scientifically speaking, mostly wishful thinking. The advent of the New Physics coupled with the New Age thinking put some muscle and credibility into the creation of the force that we are on the forefront of today.

It was Max Planck, a theoretical physicist, who discovered that the energy of heat radiation is not emitted continuously, but appears in the form of "energy packets." These energy packets were named *quanta,* by none other than Albert Einstein. Einstein boldly stated (and this was indeed VERY bold for his time) that light and every other form of electromagnetic radiation can appear as either wave or quanta (particles). This totally ransacked the mechanistic view of the universe which, up until then, matter of factly pronounced that the world was made of matter, and was also deterministic (scientifically predictable). Quantum theory swept aside all the classical concepts and "showed" that on the subatomic level there is no substance, just probabilities of interconnections. What does this mean? It means that the world is not made up of little isolated building blocks, but is a "oneness" which includes the observer! This was discovered and enumerated by Werner Heisenberg, another theoretical physicist, who announced that whether a subatomic particle was a wave or a particle was determined by the expectation of the observer! This meant the observer was a co-creator rather than just being the uninvolved spectator most scientists had always thought of themselves as being. Proposed in 1927 by Heisenberg, the Principle of Uncertainty gives evidence that the act of observation is in reality more an act of participation. What does this mean? It means that the days of a deluded, uninvolved objectivity towards life and, further, the notion that we are "visitors to the never changing universe" are over. We now enter an age where we are very, very actively involved in co-creating reality. (Read Capra's fascinating work, *The Tao of Physics,* on this.)

So from this condensed historical synopsis we add the string of dominoes from shamanism to the string of dominoes from the Quimby Bunch, which joins the string of dominoes from the Quantum Physics Gang, and you have one significant trend stream evidencing a credible and incredible paradigm power shift. We now have an historical, scientific and experiential foundation of "proof," if you will, that we are empowered and always have been, even to the point of making it true when we said we were powerless! We have <u>formally</u> moved from a totally isolated and/or victim relationship with the universe to a holistic and participative one.

This is why psychotechnological practices have come into being. These practices say, "New Age, New Rules, New Opportunities" to tinker with our universes. And there is a lot of tinkering going on! Here is a list of some of the independent psychotechnological practices that have been precipitated since the SQQ (shamanism, quimby, quantum) influences united in time (apologies to those missed):

Affirmations	Inner Alchemy
Alexander Technique	Inner Child Work
Aura Balancing	Logotherapy
Autogenic Training	Metaprogramming
Bioenergetics	Naturopathy
Biofeedback	NLP
Creative Visualization	Noetics
Cybernetics	Paradox Process
Dianetics	Past-Life Regression
Dreamwork, Lucid	Psychoimmunity
EST (The Forum)	Psychosynthesis
Feldenkrais Method	Psychotronics
Firewalking	Quantum Psychology
Guided Imagery	Rebirthing
Hakomi	Reiki
Holotropic Breathwork	Transcendental Meditation
Holodynamics	Vivation

I have suggested a more stringent definition of *Psychotechnology* in the front section of the *Phoenix Flight Manual* than has been previously used. It is capitalized when used as a noun since it is more and more apparently becoming a principled field of exploration. When used as an adjective, *psychotechnological* is not capitalized. The formalizing of the field of Psychotechnology organizes the purposes and energies for even more beneficial manifestations of empowerment for all involved. Better communications, data-gathering, networking, and an eventual cohesive philosophy of transformation can and will occur. This is one of the *raison d'etre* for this Manual. From this comes an increased ability to promote health and wealth, thereby relegating misery to the status of a free choice. Psychotechnology, then, is the science of individual empowerment—the power to create one's life in any manner one chooses.

PSYCHOTECHNOLOGY: The science of individual ability to deliberately alter moods, behaviors, and even life patterns with the optimal application of a primary thought.

With that, let's get back to the MOM and the beginning of the Phoenix Solution at Stage 5. There is no longer a need for Randy and Candy so we bid them thanks and adieu.

5. THE PROBLEM IS PASSIONATELY POSSESSED.
(Step 1 of the Phoenix Solution)

The User's Manual at the front of this volume talks about what works. In the Technical Manual we want to talk about what doesn't. We know that it is next to impossible to solve a problem that is disclaimed. So, besides the excellent ways we have already mentioned—lack of awareness, mislocating the general area needing adjustment, and a lack of internal locus of control—what are roadblocks to possession of a problem? Some rather hefty ones include: Willingness and Responsibility.

Willingness

At any moment in time, I have the potential to make many choices, to do many things—literally millions! Then why do I choose the ones I do? Why am I *willing* to only do the things I do? The old psychology called it *volition* or *will*, like it was a thing. Nobody knew where this "thing" was located or what it looked like in its pure form, but if it is a thing it must be someplace and have form, according to the same science that treated it as a thing. Quantum thinking would look at willingness as energy that is always moving in one direction or another. So, again, the real question is why in certain directions? Perhaps a look at the *contexts* of willingness will help at least display its modes of movement. Let us divide human willingness (energy) into 5 types, each having its own characteristics or dynamic patterns of response.

WILLINGNESS 1:
Innocence/curiosity>totally open>search for connection

The non-judgmental child-like state of mind which is fascinated by and accepting of sensory input while seeking for connection and exploration.

WILLINGNESS 2:
Discomfort>narrow openness>search for relief

The state of being in which one is at some level of physical/emotional/mental pain and is in need of specific relief.

WILLINGNESS 3:
Achievement>specific openness>search for completion

The need to advance in the direction of a predetermined goal in order to experience a sense of progressive movement.

WILLINGNESS 4:
Insight>variable openness>search for growth and expansion

A sudden desire to open up to new combinations of perceived reality due to a sensing of a potential to be realized.

WILLINGNESS 5:
Humility>expansive openness>affirmation

A wisdomic state of being in which one values positively all that one experiences.

It is apparent that the type of willingness determines not only the type of openness but also the length and pattern of search behavior for satisfaction as well. The nature of the goal pursued likewise varies with each type of willingness, implying, for example, that attempting to create change with a "growth" inducement (Willingness 3) will not be effective for someone coming from a "discomfort" (Willingness 2) frame of reference.

TYPE	Initial State	Openness	Goal
WILLINGNESS 1	Innocence/ Curiosity	Total	Connection
WILLINGNESS 2	Discomfort	Narrow	Relief from pain
WILLINGNESS 3	Achievement	Specific	Progress towards goal
WILLINGNESS 4	Insight	Sudden/unpredictable	Application
WILLINGNESS 5	Humility	Expansive	Universal affirmation

Willingness 1 and Willingness 5 are similar in that they are egoless states, but #1 is natural at birth and then it reappears clothed with age and experience in #5. The types do appear to naturally follow an age and stage pattern, and end up spiraling into what looks like a circle at first glance. Perhaps this explains Jesus' often quoted statement, "Except as ye become as little children, ye shall not enter the kingdom of Heaven." It is helpful to possess all

5 types of willingness and then be able to choose which one is most pertinent or preferable at any moment. Effectiveness in modifying circumstances demands willingness to do so, and the fastest route to change is the willingness to take responsibility for the situation.

Responsibility

My suspicion is that the parenting styles in our "evolved" culture have corrupted our natural sense of responsibility. John Bradshaw once said on a videotape that "No one in the United States has completed the second year of life successfully." He went on to talk about how children are seen as chattel, and are still being maimed and shaped by abusive and well-intentioned parents alike. I believe he is fairly accurate with that statement. Children are often spiritually abused by their parents in the sense that the parents are always right even when they are wrong, and our world (expectations of socially acceptable behavior in society, schools and business) is not set up to accommodate, much less affirm, children as they are. We basically force children to be and then remain dependent, when their true nature is to break free and become independent. This is also a short diagnosis for why we do not operate well societally. The natural evolution of humans in society is supposed to be something like this:

Dependence => Independence => Interdependence

Children need two things from their parents: love and protection. Children are not designed for inculcation of values, the projection of their parents' unfinished business upon them, or assembly-line schools. They are designed for freedom after a short period of getting the hang of using their wings. In my human development courses when we look at the ages and stages of life, adolescence is now extended to 22 years of age on the average (it used to be 18) because in the United States we now have more 22 year-old "kids" living at home than ever before in our history. This may be necessary in consideration of the way our society has evolved, but it certainly isn't a natural part of our genetic programming. After this extended period of dependence on one end of the continuum, and the predominance of "dysfunctional familyism" on the other end where kids do not get the proper period/type of love and protection required for healthy development, it is no surprise that we have a society of people who are either still little-kid dependent or have a warped sense of independence. This could then account for the inability for most people to move into a healthy state of interdependence where they could maintain an individual identity and yet participate productively in relationships. The fabric of our society rests totally on the interdependence abilities of its member. This, in turn, rests upon the dependent/independent skills developed during childhood.

Suggested prescription: Families should work more collaboratively to make their decisions and solve their problems. Schools should teach with more cooperative learning strategies, and society should put an end to child abuse and neglect by moving it to a top priority position now that we no longer need all that money for war weapons. (For more information on these topics refer to my three books: *The Expert Educator*; *Is Education Having A Heart Attack?...Eight Symptoms and A Plan for Rehabilitation;* and, *Assessing The Effects of Being Raised in a Dysfunctional Setting.*)

We must make a concerted effort by committing to a plan of reestablishing personal responsibility to its natural and rightful place inside our youth and ourselves. From this effort there will come many benefits and solutions to problems that keep us locked into the "Ain't It A Shame Game" as one of our major ineffective coping mechanisms.

One way we can all model this is by owning what's "bothering" us at any moment in time. Nothing upsets me except that I have drawn a line in the sand saying, "Don't cross this line or I will be upset!" We must never forget that *we are drawing the line in the sand.* We have that right. We are allowed to draw as many lines in the sand as we want. We just need to hold ourselves accountable for the lines and stop casting the blame everywhere except at ourselves. (If we find ourselves sitting in the middle of a pile of crap, guess who raked it in?) To the point of near obnoxiousness, those of us in mental and educational professions need to continually recenter our clients/customers in dealing with their present day issues by saying, "What part are you playing in this problem?" and then help them find meaningful answers— answers that will put them back in the driver's seat of their lives. Nobody can ask more of the support professions than to teach people responsibility and the tools with which to be effective in exercising that responsibility.

Conscious Connected Breathing (CCB)

A few further notes are necessary regarding CCB.

1) Conscious Connected Breathing creates instant responsibility with the first willing breath because it puts you in the driver's seat (internal locus of control) of a major life force immediately.

2) It reminds you just how much you are IN the present moment, where all choices are made.

3) Sustained CCB deliberately alters moods so that you can plant effective affirmative modifiers (Primary Domino Thoughts), and it also serves as a reminder that you can actually be in charge of how you feel!

4) CCB provides power over the unconscious and the autonomic systems of the body where a lot of energy is stored.

5) Because of all the control manifested in 1-4 above, CCB accesses positive self-esteem, confidence-building and increases success probabilities within you.

6) Your breathing acts as an emotional rheostat, like a light dimmer switch. When you don't wish to experience your emotions (suppression), you breathe shallowly and brokenly. Breathing full conscious connected breaths will put you in touch with your feelings, including the ones you have been avoiding as well as the ones that make life exciting. Say goodbye to boredom!

7) Jim Leonard—one of the greatest breathers of all time!—states in *Your Fondest Dream*: "The advanced energy flow in your body that you get from doing CCB feels wonderful. It feels great to feel your aliveness in an enhanced way."(p. 192)

8) A majority of your waste products are supposed to leave your body via your exhale. Suppressed (shallow) breathing leaves you with things you don't want in your system, and, conversely, full circular breaths freshen and invigorate your body as it is intended to be. "Runner's high" that is talked about by runners is just sustained CCB. You don't have to run to get an invigorated boost; just sit still and do CCB for about 20 minutes and see what happens.

Despite all these advantages we still forget to use CCB, especially when we most need it; therefore, constant practice and reminders are called for until this positive new habit is established. It is worth the effort many times over to reprogram this important bodily function. In my seminars CCB is always one of the top positive items written about on evaluations.

6. THE PROBLEM IS CLEARLY DEVELOPED
(Step 2 of the Phoenix Solution)

Problems are "hot." People want to dump them as fast as they arrive despite all the cliches,"Life is problems," "We grow through problems," You learn from your mistakes," "Problems build character," etc. Most of us have a hard time sitting with a problem long enough to know it well—to let it fully develop, like a photograph in the developer, gradually coming clearly into focus. Men in particular are raised to be project and problem-solver oriented as one of their main ego-strengths. There's nothing wrong with this, but sometimes the need to also hold the competitive edge sometimes rushes the process towards solution too rapidly to allow the true problem to emerge. Whoever said "Patience is a virtue" must have been talking about problem-solving, because it is certainly a good guiding principle for that scenario. Sitting quietly for five minutes and reflecting on a problem, or consciously putting a problem onto your "backburner" and sleeping on it, can often produce astounding results.

Some possible key questions to answer in developing a problem to clarity: [For group work, just change all the pronouns "I-my" to "we-our."]

1) What is the purpose in solving this problem?

2) What is the data on this problem, its characteristics, descriptors, frequency, evidence, etc.?

3) Is more data needed before the problem can be clarified? How do I get it?

4) What is my frame of reference and/or point of view on the issue?

5) Are there prejudices or biases on my part while viewing the issue?

6) What are my assumptions on this issue? Do they need verification?

7) What are possible implications and consequences of this issue?

8) Who exactly owns the problem? Who are the stakeholders and in what amount?

9) Am I the right person to be solving this problem? Do I need help with this?

There is no consistent formula for solving problems (no matter how many manuals lay out those little sequential steps), but clarity of the problem is of the essence, and some of the above questions may help clear the fog away a bit. Of critical importance is problem/issue ownership, as is asked about in 8 and 9 above. It is expected that the boundaries in some things which need changing can be hazy. It is all the more important that ownership be established in such a case. If the answer is a solid "Mine!" then the passionate possession of Stage 1 in the Phoenix Solution still holds as one moves onto Stage 3. If it is now determined that the problem is not "mine," then the problem can be surrendered to the proper authorities.

7. A CONSCIOUS COMMITMENT TO TAKE ACTION IS PRESENT. (Not a step in the Phoenix Solution)

Although this concept is critical to its success, it cannot be a distinct step of the Phoenix Solution because it is a state of being more than a state of doing, and the Phoenix Solution describes only things you can DO. A state of commitment enables the doing, but you cannot directly "do commitment." The concept of commitment is not specifically discussed in the front part of the *Phoenix Flight Manual* because the whole Manual is about removing the things that prevent, or creating the things that cause, natural commitments to occur.

Commitment is a little noticed small thing that makes big things happen, so it is very important that it be discussed here. One cannot expect a lecture on commitment to make people committed, but there are two thoughts on this that are most helpful. Sometimes it is just a matter of understanding that allows the flow of powerful natural forces to continue.

1) Commitment is persistent willingness.

Commitment in a relationship is being willing to experience all the feelings and still give the relationship top priority. Commitment to a job is continuing to give the work the same priority no matter what the emotional experiences may be. Commitment is courage: Going on despite the ominous 3 F's - Fear, Frustration, & Failure. Commitment is following through, keeping the contract, undauntedness, and/or finishing what was started. It is responsibility and reliability all rolled into one. It is a spiritual quality of the highest value. If you have friends, business associates, or a plumber who has this quality, nurture the relationship for it is one well worth having and keeping.

2) You are your commitments.

What you give priority to is who you are. This is one way to break the trance of who you fantasize about being and find out who you really are. Where do you put your energy? Energy is represented by thought-content and the subsequent behaviors. Those subsequent behaviors are represented by how you spend your time and money. Keeping a time diary and a money diary for a month gives you a reality check that is almost always eye-opening about yourself. It forces you to get honest. When I taught undergraduate psychology years ago, we used a Time Diary in Psych I and a Money Diary in Psych II to help the students grasp what their values were at the time. It was a very productive learning experience for them. It brought them face to face with the truth of their lives, thereby giving them the opportunity to rethink the directions they were heading.

Acknowledging the gravity of the concept of commitment explains some individual's inability or reluctance to be committed. Commitment is a major investment of one's life energy and, further, it holds one accountable. It says, "You can measure me by this!" It says, "I have forsaken all the other possible enterprises for this!" "This is who I am, what I value, how I spend my life, what is most important to me, and it probably doesn't agree with everyone around me, but I'm committed to this anyway." Wow. No wonder people are afraid of commitment. It makes good sense to have a sense of awe about what one commits to. But here's the paradox-clincher: As long as you are alive you are committed to something anyway! Every second you are putting your thoughts, time and money somewhere anyway. You have been committed since your brain started having thoughts in the womb! So, in another way, commitment is no big deal. The question is not whether to be committed. The question is to what should I be committed? It's all about choosing and then sticking to the choice.

One commitment choice is to be noncommittal. "I am committed to not committing!" Well, you could be a lot of fun to be around for about five minutes. You might make a good source of entertainment, but most of us wouldn't feel a sense of reliability or loyalty around you, so intimacy (the thing we all want) would be out of the question. You would also most likely be in the process of using people or being used by them most of the time. Not a healthy picture.

<u>Learning commitment</u>

How do people learn to be committed? A clue may lie in Joseph Chilton Pearce's *Magical Child...Rediscovering Nature's Plan for Our Children,* a momentous work published in 1977 that has much to say about eliminating most of our societal problems at the roots. He tells of Marcelle Geber who studied Ugandan children in an attempt to explain what accounted for them being the most developmentally advanced children in the world. While conducting a United Nations Children's Fund research project on malnutrition in Kenya and Uganda in 1956, Marcelle had discovered that Ugandan children were the most precocious, brilliant and gifted children anywhere, including being months ahead of American and European children. What she found were two early childhood practices that set them apart; first, they were born naturally at home usually by the mother herself, and then were carried in a sling next to the mother's breast continuously. The children fed whenever they wanted, and were awake a surprising amount of time—alert, watchful, happy, calm. They virtually never cried. Secondly, [and very important for our purposes] the Ugandan infants were bonded to their mothers in a way that their mothers sensed their needs before the need had to be expressed by crying. The mother responded to the infant's every gesture and assisted the child in any and every move that was undertaken; thus, *every move initiated by the child ended in success.*

The italics were added by me. I don't think Joseph was paying that much attention to this part of Geber's study, as he was more interested in making a point about natural births vs. hospital births. And I suppose I wouldn't pay that much attention to it either, just being one anecdotal line from one study, except when I couple this with my psychotherapeutic practice with hundreds and hundreds of people suffering the results of dysfunctional upbringing and note the one symptom every one of them had: a warped sense of commitment. They either couldn't focus on positive goals long enough to manifest them, or the opposite was true in that they were compulsively committed to destructive practices such as alcohol and other drugs, perfectionism, workaholism, co-dependent relationships, etc. Often, the whole "cure" for my clients has been discovering their sense of mission(s) and clearing away the things which get in the way. Once that was done, most had no need to come into my office, except when "new" old wreckage from the past would show up.

The point being made here is that children need to meet with success in their child's play. If we have a home (and school) environment that assists children in completing their efforts with a sense of personal achievement we probably would not have to worry about commitment in adults. It's a good thought, but suppose this background doesn't exist? Are there other things that can be done to install commitment? Yes.

1) By modeling admirable people who are committed.

Likable and respectable role models, heroes, mentors, and even fictional characters who demonstrate commitment teach us well. We hear the stories like Dorothy Hamil's, who practiced her ice skating eight hours a day, six days a week and then, as a child, would cry for the few minutes she had to leave the ice every four hours so the ice machine could resurface the rink. Or our favorite musician talking about the years of disciplined practice it took to become the "overnight success." Or comedian Jim Carey talking about doing stand-up for ten long years before he was "noticed" and began getting multimillion dollar contracts for movie performances. Examples such as these have the potential to become a Primary Domino Thought for commitment.

2) By seeing that our rewards for being committed are bigger than for not being committed.

In conjunction with seeing this same thing in role models, how about learning from our own experience? We see the payoffs in our dedicated efforts are more rewarding to us in the way we feel about ourselves, the raising of our self-esteem, and possibly even material gains. I won a substantial amount of money in a lottery that I didn't usually play just because I committed to following my "silly hunch." The lesson plans in the courses I teach at the college that are the most successful are the ones I commit to preparing adequately. The Gillette Manor (the antebellum building that houses our home and offices) is beautiful now because we committed to restoring it over a three year period. These things make me feel good—they pay off—so because of this, I am more inclined towards commitment than away from commitment.

3) By reflecting and acknowledging what we have learned from commitment experiences.

Can we learn from reflection? You bet, if we would just take the time to do it. There is a school inside of us that is partially explainable by biochemistry and psychology, i.e., we learn from our stored past memories in combination with daily experiences. There is another part of this school that is a mystery—we don't know where these insights and intuitions come from! All we need to know is that they do happen. All we need to do is sit, breathe, be receptive, and wait with the expectation of learning something. A client's first experience with this was to exclaim, "Dr.

Dallmann-Jones, it was like learning from the air around me!" Reflectiveness is a skill that can be learned, and a very profitable one. In *Is Education Having A Heart Attack?* I mention the ideal school curriculum should be the 4 R's:

Resourceful: Acquire the traditional 3 R's, informational and technological skill-building, and utilizing to capacity all 7 of the multiple intelligences.

Respectful: Learning how to be non-abusive and non-neglectful by feeling good about oneself, sensing the pain of causing pain in others, and realizing the poor short- and long-term payoffs in being disrespectful.

Responsible: Taking charge of your life and being self-reliant and empowered.

Reflective: Becoming metacognitive, or thinking about thinking while you are thinking. Teaching yourself. Learning from the air.

8. A SPECIFIC MODIFIER IS DEVELOPED
(Step 3 of the Phoenix Solution)

This is where the Phoenix Solution gets a tad technical. There's just no way around it. We are turning around the world here, putting ourselves at cause rather than effect in ways never consciously dreamed of before. It's obviously going to create some mind-torque to bring this transformative state about, so one must commit to indulge and endure the science if one wants it's benefits.

If we have learned one thing from eastern traditions, we have learned that the mind makes a great slave, but not always so good a master. Step 3 concerns putting the mind to work as the laborer for which it was intended. How can we make the mind effective at carrying out our plans?

Imagine that you want to construct a building as your end product. You have hired workers and meet them the first day at the construction site at 7:00 a.m. You say to them, "Build me a building on this lot someday," and then you leave with no further instructions. What kind of product will you get? Let's take it further. You come back every week and notice the dismal results, and rant and rave about the "poor help these days," how "nothing works in my life," and "you better do what I want or else!" and then leave again without listening to the workers. As the days go by, you feel more and more frustrated, more disappointed, and maybe even more fatigued about your project. Despite all this energy 'going into the project', you sadly note that it still isn't coming about like you wanted it to, surrender to a sense of depression, and finally just scrap the whole affair. You nurse your wound and save up your energy for a while, and then once again remind yourself that you should get going with something worthwhile in your life. You decide to start a new project. You buy another lot, hire some new workers, meet them on-site at 7:00 a.m. and say, "Build me a building on this lot someday," and then you leave with no further instructions.

Consciousness (a larger universal source of power in each of us) can do many things. One of its components is a little engine, best known as a brain encapsulated "mind." The mind, too, has many capabilities, but those capabilities are best served by a certain type of very specific instruction. If you say to the mind, "I want to be slim/wealthy/healthy/smart/etc.," and walk away and expect the mind to do something with that vagueness, then you have some learning to do. The Phoenix Solution is a very specific way of getting maximum performance from your mind-engine. Learn it well, and the mind will deliver unto you what you want, as a good paid employee should.

Formulation

Previously in Step 2 of the Phoenix Solution, the thing needing changing (problem) was developed and clarified. If done well, that essential step develops a very clear straightforward 'statement of the problem.' An extremely essential component is the transition from the statement of the problem to the Primary Domino Thought. This is one of the things that makes the Phoenix Solution so unique, and it is accomplished in two stages.

Stage 1 Formulation: Constructing a Modifier

In the first stage the clarified problem is transitioned into a positive statement, identified as the *modifier*. The *modifier* in the Phoenix Solution is an *affirmation*, a positive mirror image of the problem statement. There are different types and qualities of affirmations, and some can be very powerful just by themselves. Affirmations are positive thoughts which can be written, read and/or spoken. The purpose of an affirmation is to replace a negative, self-abusive, stress-producing, disempowering thought with a positive, self-enhancing, empowering one. Since all behavior begins with thoughts it appears to be a good investment to make sure the roots of behavior are healthy and enjoyable.

GUIDELINES FOR CREATING AFFIRMATIONS

1. **Personal:** You can only affirm for yourself. Do not try to affirm qualities or changes in other people to correct or alter situations you cannot control. In developing affirmations, you are changing your creative *modus operandi* through personal positive statements. In most cases an affirmation should be an "I" statement.

2. **Positive:** Write out affirmations. Utilize positive language in development. Do not describe what you are trying to move away from or eliminate. Do not use words like *not, never, none,* etc.

3. **Present tense:** Affirmations should be stated in the present tense. The reason present tense is used in describing affirmations is that this is the only time frame in which the subconscious operates. Avoid using future tense phrases such as "I will..." or "Someday..." "I'm going to..."

4. **Indicate achievement:** Do not indicate the ability, "I can," in your affirmation, because this will not produce change. <u>You already have the ability</u>. What you must indicate concretely is actual achievement. For example, begin statements with "I am..." and "I have..."

5. **Action words:** Describe the activity you are affirming in terms that create pictures of you performing in an easy and anxiety-free manner. Your subconscious actions should be described by statements that start with: "I easily," "I quickly," "I enjoy," "I love to," "I thrive on," and "I show."

6. **Emotion words:** Try to put as much excitement in the wording of your affirmations as you can by vividly stating your behavior in colorful terms. Words that spark an emotional picture in your subconscious help to make the experience in your affirmation more believable and attractive.

7. **Accuracy:** It is important for you to affirm only as high as you can honestly imagine yourself becoming or performing. The rule of thumb is to not overshoot (too unrealistic to believe) or undershoot (sell yourself short). Just hold a clear and vivid picture of the end result you want to accomplish. Being accurate does not mean being perfectionistic. Your investment is not in perfection, but in excellence.

8. **Privacy:** Your affirmations are personal and should be for yourself only. Others may constantly try to remind you of your old ways without really meaning to hold you back. Part of the power of the affirmational atmosphere is that people around you may get "upset" (feel out of control) when you start changing and growing. To restore their feelings of internal control and predictability others may subconsciously want to keep you the way you were, even if you were unhappy or unhealthy.

Stage 2 Formulation: Shaping the Modifier into a Primary Domino Thought (PDT)

Once the *modifier* in the form of an affirmation is constructed to the specifications, it must be compacted into a representative Primary Domino Thought (PDT). Repeating affirmations is effective, but writing them repeatedly is even more effective because it keeps the mind focused and the body involved as well. The Phoenix Solution goes beyond this second level of effectiveness into an even more potent catalytic vehicle, the PDT. As an example, you just read "PDT" and you knew what it meant, yet it occupied less than 25% of the space and only about 33% of your reading time compared to "Primary Domino Thought." So, a PDT is a more potent (efficient and effective) form of an affirmation. You might say that a Primary Domino Thought is an "affirmation magnum."

The Primary Domino Thought is a much shortened representative version of the affirmation-based *modifier*. The PDT should be "catchy" to the user. "Catchy" means that it has some sort of very subjective appeal to the user. The appeal is something that sort of clicks in when one finds it. Although it might not mean a thing to anyone else, for the user it encompasses the *modifier* and more. It has an emotional tug to it, an encompassing wholeness about it, perhaps even a gut-level impact that this is the one. It is important to note that the PDT can be in different forms:

a) linguistic = a word, phrase, or acronym
b) numerical = single number, number phrase, or formula
c) symbols = yin-yang, flag; ♡; ☺; ☥; ☆; ┏; ₤; etc., etc.
d) photographic snapshot
e) animated film clip
f) abstraction of swirling colors, sliding geometric figures, etc.
g) any combination of the above.

The only criteria for a good PDT is that it mentally represents the *modifier* and has an added subjective feeling of identification with it. Creativity in brevity is also encouraged in order to maximize impact. Telephone numbers are 7 digits long because that is the maximum convenient length for easy memory recall. One reason why sentence-length mental affirmations are not as effective is because the "string" is too long for the easy and quick access time mandated for the subconscious work of restructuring neural pathways. Likewise, meaningful brevity in PDTs is naturally congruent with the accelerative flavor that drives the purposes of psychotechnologies—shortening the time and lessening the amount of resources needed to bring about productive change.

9. THE MODIFIER IS APPLIED
(Step 4 of the Phoenix Solution)

The proverbial moment of truth is the actual application of the PDT. The process is very well-detailed in the front of the Manual, but due to the unique aspects of the Phoenix Solution at this point in the MOM process, some expansions might be helpful.

Creating the good moment

It is our natural tendency to only think about change when things are not going as well. When content or happy we just want to coast. The Phoenix Solution urges investor-type thinking. When things are going well is the optimal time to implant PDT *modifiers*, so conditioning the mind to notice these golden moments is imperative. But, the big question is, if I don't 'feel good' do I have to wait in order to utilize the Phoenix Solution? No. You can create the 'good moment' much as a farmer creates good soil in preparation for planting. Conscious Connected Breathing (CCB) is one very quick way to do this. Norman Cousins' work at UCLA and elsewhere has clearly shown that laughter can produce auspicious physiological changes, thereby creating that 'fertile soil' needed for effective transitions. Pleasant memories quickly give evidence of positive physiological shifts, again giving rise to the opportune teachable moment of transition.

Recontextualization

CCB, humor, and pleasant memories really fall under the umbrella rubric of shifting contexts or *recontextualization*, or the ability to choose another way to regard some thing or event. Jim Leonard, the creator of VIVATION™, calls recontextualization "integration."

"The shift from a negative context to a positive context is called *integration* because something you had held in opposition to your sense of well-being you now integrate into your sense of well-being. If you are focusing on how awful it is to have only $1000 you are making your money wrong. If you shift [your context] to gratitude that you have any money at all you integrate the money back into your sense of well-being again." (Leonard, p. 174)

The logical dynamics of recontextualization are as follows:

1. Our value-judgments determine the way in which we view things.

2. Value-judgments make the difference in whether the glass is appreciated for being half-full or lamented over for being half-empty.

3. The way in which we view things/events determines the mind-body (emotional) reaction we will have to those things/events.

4. Negative value-judging is either fear-based, or a bad habit formed in fearful circumstances, and results in declarations of "make-wrong.

5. Positive value-judging is love-based and results in declarations of "make-right."

6. We create an internal momentary state of either Heaven or Hell with our value-judging.

7. *Recontextualization* is the ability to shift the way we view things.

8. *Recontextualization* is a way we can begin to <u>deliberately</u> create our own internal state of being.

Recontextualization is not glib "positive thinking," as some people advocate. It is not about hopeful, wishful, or magical thinking. Any thing or event can be seen in literally an unlimited number of contexts, both subjectively negative and positive to us. Recontextualization is about making a deliberate choice to see some thing or event in a positive way as opposed to a negative way.

Practice brings this home.

Event: Flat tire on your car on the open highway
Negative Contexts: Inconvenience; late; expensive; stuck; alone; dangerous; frightening; confused; frustrated; _____; _____; _____.
Positive Contexts: Finally use my AAA benefits; meet new people; challenge; learn new skills; good story for later; exhibit my independence; exhibit my dependence; _____; _____; _____.

Event: No money in my account
Negative Contexts: Broke; starve; embarrassing; stupid; again!; bad luck; frustrated; _____; _____; _____.
Positive Contexts: Humility; better understanding of poverty; not overdrawn; money goes <u>and</u> comes again; focus on what I bought; stay home and meditate; _____; _____; _____.

Event: Terminal cancer diagnosis
Negative Contexts: Death; pain; fear; unknown; medical tests; drain on my family; expensive; _____; _____; _____.

Positive Contexts: Live for the moment; openness to love and support; spiritual development; make peace with things and people; learning experience; finally overcome fear of dying; make new acquaintances; ultimate challenge; _____; _____; _____.

Now, for practice, you do some:

Event:
Negative Contexts:
Positive Contexts:

Event:
Negative Contexts:
Positive Contexts:

Event:
Negative Contexts:
Positive Contexts:

Recontextualization profoundly alters your view of things, the way you feel in your body, and your predominant emotions, which means it profoundly changes your life in the moment—*exactly the right time to implant a PDT.* Learning to implant PDTs at opportune moments is the height of intelligent living.

Generating the visualization, emotion and physical sensation of accomplishment

The action step needed to impress your PDT on the subconscious is a combination of imaging and feeling processes.

Imaging

As you implant the PDT, you should be vividly picturing and experiencing yourself clearly as having already accomplished the change you want, or the end result you intend to create. Through this experimental visualization, you are displacing old self-images with new pictures of how you want to feel and act. Remember, you are practicing and experiencing the change consciously to begin with, but through your picturing you are turning your expectations over to the subconscious, and very quickly you will begin moving easily and naturally to your new performance reality.

Feeling

Feeling the emotion that accompanies the results you want is important for maximizing impact. Gather up the feelings, based on your five senses, that you know will accompany the accomplished goal, and enjoy them in vivid detail each time you imprint your modifying PDT. The PDT will affect your system in a positive way in direct proportion to the frequency you use vividness in imaging and emotional involvement. Generally speaking the imprinting of a PDT can be broken down as follows:

    Just reading it: 10% impact
    Reading and imaging it: 55% impact
    Reading, imaging and feeling it: 100% impact
    (Courtesy The Pacific Institute, Seattle, Washington)

Imprinting through visualizing the right picture with emotion speeds the change process!

Your purpose in using this technique is to overlay the current images in your subconscious with a predetermined outcome in the form of new images and emotions. For example, in weight loss, you are changing the "picture" of how you look or how much you should weigh. Once you have programmed in the new picture, you cannot tolerate the old, and your creative subconscious helps you reach the new picture. It may be through dieting, exercise, changing habits, or some combination of actions, but those new patterns will emerge naturally once the new PDT is thoroughly implanted and, any unwanted old ones are removed.

APPENDIX II

The E.R.P. List

A Psychotechnique For Erasing Destructive Patterns

ERASING DESTRUCTIVE PATTERNS—The E.R.P. List

Change is a constant part of our thinking as evidenced by many of our frequently used inner and outer dialogues:

"Things are moving so fast these days."
"I wish I could change my finances/weight/habits/relationship/ feelings/job/etc."
"We have got to quit/move/beef-up/rearrange/start/be more careful with/etc."
"I can't wait until..."
"If only..."

Sounds as if we are always dissatisfied, but perhaps, more accurately, we are *lamenting* that we just don't know *how* to change things permanently. The lack of ability to bring about permanent change can be a critical deficit when it involves dealing with life-damaging habits. At the Institute for Transformational Studies we have evolved several techniques for accelerating permanent recovery from unhealthy patterns. Some are complex, such as The WINDOORS Program for Adult Survivors, the Phoenix Solution, and the live-in Personal Intensives, but some, such as the ERP List, can be easily communicated in just a few pages.

It can be a rough journey merely getting to the deciding point of clearing one's life of a destructive pattern, but sooner or later one says something to the effect: *"These cigarettes have got to go!"* or *"Apparently I have no good sense when it comes to eating."* or *"If I don't get out of this relationship I'm going to* [do something drastic].*"* First, we begin by threatening ourselves into quitting the habit; secondly, we screw up the courage to quit; thirdly, we quit, usually with great trepidation; and, finally after a period of time we return (relapse) to the habit with great anguish and guilt. Sound familiar? We have all experienced this frustrating cycle with ourselves and/or our clients. There is a culprit that, like a powerful magnet, brings us back to our destructive pattern. It is helpful as well as relieving to name this gremlin within.

Often the reason we return to nasty habits and unhealthy practices or relationships is a phenomenon known as *euphoric recall*. When we finally begin to abstain from a destructive pattern we do so with all of the good reasons right in front of us. As time passes the negative aspects of the destructive pattern that brought us to the point of abstention begin to dim, while the pieces of the habit we enjoyed begin to grow brighter. Eventually the favorable aspects, although fewer in number, appear to outweigh the unfavorable aspects, and we "relapse" back into the destructive pattern. This relapse is usually accompanied by a lowering of self-esteem and, more importantly, the lessening of willingness to try again the next time we decide the negatives of a habit outweigh the positives.

To counter this natural recurrence of desire in my clients (and myself) I developed a technique known as the ERP List, or Euphoric Recall Prevention List. It works very simply and effectively if we have two capabilities: (1) Willingness to quit and, (2) Ability to stick to a commitment. If these are present in even small amounts the technique works wonders. The ERP List itself facilitates commitment. Willingness is the key issue, and not much is known about it.

Willingness

If an individual is not *willing* to change there is not much hope for success—BUT we can enhance the amount of willingness by bringing about more awareness of its dynamics.

The dynamics of willingness

At the Institute of Transformational Studies we have identified and dissected five distinct types of willingness, each having its own specifications and applications. Willingness is the root environment of the human motivation to do anything. Not thoroughly understanding willingness undermines most attempts at change.

Change that originates within the self is known as volition or *will*. Without willingness not much happens since humans are made from molecules and are, therefore, somewhat subject to the laws of physics. The law of inertia states: "That which is at rest (or in motion) remains at rest (or in motion) until some force operates upon it." Volition is difficult to define since, "*Before willingness there is just 'energy at rest'*," i.e. energy doing nothing but maintaining the status quo. And that is what humans usually do —they *maintain* until one type of willingness or another raises its head and provides the impetus for change. The five types of willingness are numbered below as W1-W5. It is intriguing that they roughly correlate with stages of human development. (These are repeated from the detailed description on page 155.)

The Five Root Environments of Human Change

WILLINGNESS 1:
Innocence/curiosity>total openness>search for connection

The non-judgmental child-like state of mind which is fascinated by and accepting of sensory input while seeking for connection and exploration.

WILLINGNESS 2:
Discomfort>narrow openness>search for relief

The state of being in which one is at some level of physical/ emotional/mental pain and is in need of specific relief.

WILLINGNESS 3:
Achievement>specific openness>search for completion

The need to advance in the direction of a predetermined goal in order to experience a sense of progressive movement.

WILLINGNESS 4:
Insight>variable openness>search for growth and expansion

A sudden desire to open up to new combinations of perceived reality due to a sensing of a potential to be realized.

WILLINGNESS 5:
Humility>expansive openness>affirmation

A wisdomic state of being in which one values positively all that one experiences.

Most of us seem mainly motivated by avoidance of painful consequences as we master lower needs (food, water, warmth, companionship, etc.) and feel secure in them. Until then we often develop blinders to our potential as an independently empowered entity because we are outwardly focused, i.e., we have an external locus of control, and are consequently *disempowered* (which sounds suspiciously like "disemboweled").

One way out of this dilemma is to shift a desire for change from a demand to one of preference. It is significantly less stressful to say "*I prefer to abstain from...*" as opposed to "*I have to abstain from...*" This is because the second statement includes desperation and resentment. The first statement is imbued with the freedom to choose and have control over one's life. It is preferable to upgrade demands to preferences as it places one in an adult to adult relationship with self as opposed to a parent-child relationship with self based on "shoulds," "havetos," "musts," "gottas," and "oughtas." These very common negative methods of self-motivation establish the pattern of alleviating discomfort with even more discomforting motivational systems. This will create further wounding, rather than relief. A tragic result of this can be the heaping of more compulsive behaviors in order to alleviate the added pain!

Preferences have to do with our desires to change various aspects of ourselves mentally, emotionally, physically or spiritually. The reasons we may prefer self-change are numerous and can include the perceived need to:

    a) be better equipped to achieve a goal
    b) repair damage from the past
    c) feel invigorated
    d) have more fun
    e) be creative
    f) be challenged to actualize potentialities
    g) increase one's effectiveness
    h) give a gift to oneself, another, or society.

It is much easier to successfully launch permanent change from a preferential state than from a demand state. Encouraging the upgrading of willingness from W2 to W3 (W4 will then, interestingly enough, occur naturally) will lower emotional resistance, alleviate potential distress, and encourage self-responsibility in problem-solving. At this point we can successfully launch into the powerful psychotechnique affectionately known as the ERP List.

****

THE ERP LIST

The next time you are seriously willing to leave your destructive pattern:

1) Print a clearly stated and numbered list of every reason for being disgusted with your habit, practice, or relationship. Include the most personal and nit-picky reasons, as well as the obvious ones. Take some time with this. Don't leave anything out—the longer the list the better. Do not show this list to anyone, ever. (Why? Because if you know somebody is going to see it, you may not allow yourself to write some of the better reasons!)

2) At the bottom of the list, write down the financial penalty you are going to pay if you violate your agreement with yourself. This should be equivalent to $1 for every $1000 you grossed last year, i.e., if you made $100,000 your penalty is $100.

3) Carry the list with you for one month and refer to it everyday at least once, and also every time the "urge" hits you. If the object of your addiction is extremely handy (easily acquired anywhere) like cigarettes, food, alcohol, shopping, etc., or by phone (ex-lover or bookie) then carry your list for 12 months. You may want to laminate it.

4) If you decide to give in to your urge, first immediately pay your penalty by writing a check to your favorite charity, and mail it or, if you are in a hurry, set the proper amount of $$$ on fire in a sink.

5) Then go ahead and indulge—you paid for it!

6) Sign the following:

"*Without fail, I pledge to pay the penalty every time I indulge.*"

(Signed)　　　　　　　　　　(Date)

****

This is a most effective and succinct technique. I still receive thanks from former students and clients for this simple little method: The ERP List.

APPENDIX III

Establishing Purpose

Entering the 21st Century...

ON PURPOSE

Jim Leonard & Anthony S. Dallmann-Jones, Ph.D.

If you do not know your purpose, then your life will not be determined by you. Not to worry, people will, of course, find a use for you. But if you do not know your purpose, you will adopt theirs since any purpose is better than no purpose. Unfortunately, this means that you will not feel very fulfilled and patterns of low self-esteem will surely permeate your life. Without a sense of purpose you have only the alternatives of conformity or rebellion, neither of which is deeply satisfying.

There is an alternative to conformity or rebelliousness: Self-directedness. A self-directed person knows his or her own purpose and does not look to other people for definition. Only through self-directedness can fulfillment be found. The rebel and conformist are always plagued by profound questions about whether they are doing the right thing with their lives. The self-directed person is empowered and experiences certainty.

It is also extremely difficult to make any major decision in a meaningful way without knowing your purpose. Compared to knowing what your purpose is, all other decisions are trivial. Your purpose is not something that you achieve once and then you are finished; it is something you express continuously, giving meaning to goals throughout your life. Your purpose puts your entire life into perspective.

If you do not know your purpose, you can discover it by performing the following process.

1. If you had the power to make your world any way at all, how would you choose it to be? Write this down in 20 words or less, utilizing positive language entirely.

2. Make List #1: 10 things you like about yourself in noun-based language. [my good looks; my speaking ability; my ability to memorize; etc.]

3. From List #1 circle 3 or 4 that are the most significant about you.

4. Make List #2: Ten activities you enjoy engaging in as an expression of the 3 or 4 things you listed above. These should be gerunds ending in -ing. [singing; debating with politicians; painting; cooking; presenting ideas; etc.]

5. From List #2 circle 3 or 4 that can make the biggest contribution to making the world more like the ideal you described in Step One.

6. Create your Purpose by writing out the following sentence, filling in the blanks with the selection from List #1, then List #2, then your ideal world.

"My purpose is to use my _____, _____, and _____, by_____ing, _____ ing, and _____ing so that_____."

7. Polish your grammar until your statement makes good sense to you.

****

Don't worry if your purpose(s) doesn't seem to exactly fit you at first. This is not unusual. It helps to do this every day for a week until you feel in your heart that "This is it!" Remember, this is an experience concerned with the trajectory of your life, so be willing to take your time and get it just right for you. It is strongly suggested you do this for any important projects in which you decide to invest your energy. It will make your projects more meaningful, enjoyable, enthusiastic and effective because you will be clear on what you are doing and why. Most importantly, you will be at cause rather than at effect—which is how you were designed to be.

BIBLIOGRAPHY

Allen, James. *As A Man Thinketh.* Stamford, CT. Longmeadow Press, 1993.

Armstrong, Thomas. *7 Kinds of Smart.* New York: Penguin. 1993.

Bennett, Hal Zina & Sparrow, Susan. *Follow Your Bliss.* New York: Avon Books, 1990.

Benz, Dyrian & Weiss, Halko. *To The Core of Your Experience.* Charlottesville, VA: Luminas Press, 1989.

Biffle, Christopher. *The Castle of The Pearl.* New York: Harper & Row, 1990.

Bradshaw, John. *Healing The Shame That Binds You.* Videotape Presentation, PBS. 1991.

Campbell, Peter A. & McMahhon, Edwin M. *Bio-Spirituality: Focusing As A Way To Grow.* Chicago: Loyola University Press, 1985.

Capra, Fritjof. *The Tao of Physics.* Boston: Shambhala,1991.

Carlsen, Mary B. *Meaning-Making: Therapeutic Processes in Adult Development.* New York: w.w. Norton & Co.,1988.

Chopra, Deepak. *Unconditional Life: Discovering the Power to Fulfill Your Dreams.* New York: Bantam, 1992.

_____. [Anything written by Deepak is golden.]

Cousins, Norman. *Head First...The Biology of Hope.* New York: E. P. Dutton, 1989.

Dallmann-Jones, A. S. & The Black River Group. *The Expert Educator...A Reference Manual of Teaching Strategies for Quality Education.* Fond du Lac, WI: Three Blue Herons Publishing, Inc., 1994.

Dallmann-Jones, A. S. & Osterhaus, R. *Is Education Having A Heart Attack...Eight Symptoms and A Plan for Rehabilitation.* Fond du Lac, WI: Three Blue Herons Pub., Inc., 1994.

Dallmann-Jones, A. S. *Resolving Unfinished Business.* Fond du Lac, WI: Three Blue Herons Pub., Inc., 1995.

Dossey, Larry, M.D. *Space, Time & Medicine.* Boston: New Science Library, 1982.

Eliade, Mircea. *Shamanism: Archaic Techniques of Ecstasy.* Princeton, N.J.: Princeton University Press. 1964

Ellis, Albert & Harper, Robert. *A Guide To Rational Living.* No. Hollywood, CA: Wilshire Book Co., 1973.

Ferguson, Marilyn. *The Aquarian Conspiracy: Personal and Social Transformation in Our Time.* New York: J. P. Tarcher. 1980.

FM-2030. *Are You A Transhuman?* New York: Warner Bros., 1989.

Gawain, Shakti. *Creative Visualization.* New York: Bantam Books, 1985.

_____. *The Path of Transformation.* Mill Valley, CA: Nataraj Publishing, 1993.

Geber, Marcelle. "The Psycho-Motor Development of African Children in the First Year and the Influence of Maternal Behavior." *Journal of Social Psychology*, No. 47 (1958): 185-195.

Gershon, David & Straub, Gail. *Empowerment.* New York: Dell, 1989.

Gleick, James. *Chaos: Making A New Science.* New York: Penguin, 1987.

Goswami, Amit. *The Self-Aware Universe.* New York: G. P. Putnam's Sons, 1993.

Grof, Stanislav & Binnet, Hal Z. *The Holotropic Mind.* New York: HarperCollins, 1992.

Hall, Edward T. *Beyond Culture.* New York: Doubleday, 1981.

Harvey, Bill. *Mind Magic.* New York: Unlimited Publishing, 1982.

Hay, Louise. *The Power Is Within You.* Carson, CA: Hay House, Inc.,1991.

Helmstetter, Shad. *Choices.* New York: Pocket Books, 1989.

Helmstetter, Shad. *What To Say When You Talk To Yourself.* New York: Pocket Books, 1982.

Herbert, Nick. *Elemental Mind*. New York: Penguin, 1993.
Howard, Vernon. *The Power of Your Supermind*. Marina del Ray, CA: DeVorss & Co., 1975.
Hua-Ching Ni. *Internal Alchemy*. Santa Monica, CA: The Shrine of the Eternal Breath of Tao, 1992.
Johanson, Greg & Kurtz, Ron. *Grace Unfolding: Psychotherapy in the Spirit of Tao-te Ching*. New York: Bell Tower, 1991.
Kenyon, Tom. *Brain States*. Naples, FL: United States Publishing, 1994.
Langer, Ellen. *Mindfulness*. New York: Addison-Wesley Pub. Co., Inc. 1989.
Leonard, Jim. *Your Fondest Dream*. Cincinnati: AVP Publishing, 1989.
Leonard, Jim & Laut, Phil. *Vivation: The Science of Enjoying All of Your Life*. Cincinnati: AVP Publishing, 1991.
Lilly, John & Lilly, Antonietta. *The Dyadic Cyclone*. New York: Simon & Schuster, 1976.
_____. [Anything written by John Lilly]
Lynch, Dudley & Kordis, Paul L. *Strategy of the Dolphin: Scoring A Win in A Chaotic World*. New York: Wm. Morrow & Co., 1988.
Maltz, Maxwell. *The Magic Power of Self-Image Psychology*. New York: Pocket Books, 1964.
Maslow, Abraham. *The Farther Reaches of Human Nature*. New York: Viking. 1971.
Millman, Dan. *The Way of The Peaceful Warrior*. Tiburon, CA: H.J. Kramer, Inc., 1984.
Moore, Thomas. *Care of The Soul*. New York: HarperCollins Publishers, 1992.
Peale, Norman Vincent. *You Can If You Think You Can*. Carmel, NY: Guideposts Assoc., Inc., 1974.
Pearce, Joseph C. *Magical Child*. Toronto: Clarke, Irwin & Co., 1977.
Penrose, Roger. *The Emperor's New Mind*. New York: Penguin Books, 1989.

Robbins, Tom. *Jitterbug Perfume.* New York: Bantam, 1985.
Robinson, Bryan. *Heal Your Self-Esteem: Recovery From Addictive Thinking.* Deerfield Beach, FL: Health Communications, Inc., 1981.
Shultz, J. Kennedy. *You Are The Power.* Carson, CA: Hay House, 1993.
Small, Jacquelyn. *Transformers: The Therapists of the Future.* Marina Del Ray, CA: DeVorss & Co., 1982.
Smothermon, Ron. *Transforming # 1.* San Francisco: Context Publications, 1982.
Spencer-Brown, G. *Laws of Form.* New York: E. P. Dutton, 1979.
Talbot, Michael. *The Holographic Universe.* New York: HarperCollins, 1991.
Tae Yun Kim. *Seven Steps To Inner Power.* San Rafael, CA:New World Library, 1991.
Thompson, William I. *Imaginary Landscape: Making Worlds of Myth and Science.* New York: St. Martin's Press, 1989.
Paul, Richard. *Critical Thinking: What Every Person Needs To Survive In A Rapidly Changing World.* Santa Rosa, CA: Foundation for Critical Thinking, 1992.
Smith, Lester. *Inner Adventures.* Wheaton, IL: The Theosophical Publishing House, 1988.
Woolf, V. Vernon. *Holodynamics.* New York: Harbinger House, 1990.
Watts, Alan. *Cloud-Hidden, Whereabouts Unknown.* New York: Pantheon Books, 1973.
_____. [Anything else written by Alan, ever.]
Wegner, Daniel. *White Bears & Other Unwanted Thoughts.* New York: Viking, 1989.
Wilde, Stuart. *Affirmations.* Taos, NM: White Dove, 1987.
_____. [Anything else written by Stuart, ever.]
Zukav, Gary. *The Seat of The Soul.* New York: Simon & Schuster, 1990.

INDEX

9 Approaches to Life 144, 145
Abraham Maslow 131
Accuracy 116, 147, 172
Accurate Assessment 71, 75-77
Affirmations 60, 152, 170-173
Albert Einstein 8, 151
Alexander Technique 152
Aquarian Conspiracy 148, 198
Aura Balancing 152
Autogenic Training 152
Avoidance 56, 68, 76, 136, 137, 186
Awareness 45, 47, 49, 101, 102, 116, 119, 130, 133, 136, 137,
142, 154, 184
Bioenergetics 152
Biofeedback 152
Boundaries 33, 36, 45, 81, 162
Choice 13, 33, 38, 44, 58, 62, 63, 66, 81, 100-102, 153, 164,
165, 177
Comfort Zone 14, 40, 43-45, 84, 92, 110
Confrontation 136
Consciousness 33, 47-49, 63, 100-102, 119, 139, 149, 170
Conscious Connected Breathing ... 53, 61, 64-67, 70, 76, 96, 101,
105, 107, 108, 111, 121, 139, 159, 175
Contentment 130, 132-137
Contexts 99, 106, 113, 122, 154, 175, 177, 178
Courage 17, 163, 183
Co-dependency 45
Creative Visualization 152, 198
Cybernetics 152
Delusion 16, 37, 136, 137
Demands 55-57, 157, 187
Denial 54, 61, 136, 137

Dependence 157, 158, 177
Dianetics 152
Dishonesty 30, 75
Dissociation 136
Dynamics of Problems 71
Dysfunctional Familyism 158
Emotion-sensation 103, 108
Empowerment 17, 20, 22, 35-37, 60, 119, 124, 153
ERP List 183, 184, 188, 189
Euphoric Recall Prevention 184
Extraction 102, 103, 107, 111
Fears 5, 11, 14, 76
Feeling 26, 30, 41, 61, 62, 86, 96, 104-106, 108,
110-112, 131, 133, 168, 173, 179
Feldenkrais Method 152
Firewalking 152
Five Steps of the Phoenix Solution 47, 49, 50, 148
Formulation 8, 89, 90, 170, 172
Frederick Herzberg 131
George Bernard Shaw 16
Gillette Manor 167, 201
Good Moment 99, 105, 107, 113, 122, 175
Guided Imagery 152
Guidelines for Creating Affirmations 171
Guidelines for Great Modifiers 89, 91
Hakomi 139, 152
History of Psychotechnology 19, 20, 148
Holodynamics 152
Holotropic Breathwork 139, 152
Humor 95, 99, 106, 113, 122, 175
Hypnosis 139, 149
Illusion 136, 137
Imagination 48
Imaging 179
Implant 102-104, 107, 108, 110, 114, 175, 178, 179

Independence 81, 157, 158, 177
Inner Child Work 152
Insane 14, 15, 137
Institute for Transformational Studies 118, 183, 201-203
Integration 175, 176
Interdependence 157, 158
Jim Leonard 160, 175, 193
KITA 131
Limits 33, 36, 45, 77, 137, 140
Listing Method 71, 82, 83, 86, 87
Locus of Control 33, 35-37, 56, 130, 133, 135, 143, 144, 146, 154, 159, 186
Logotherapy 152
Map of Modification 127, 129-131, 133-135, 148
Marcelle Geber 165
Marilyn Ferguson 148
Max Planck 150
Meditation 21, 69, 112, 139, 152
Metacognition 24, 168
Metaprogramming 152
Modifier 89-97, 108, 109, 115, 116, 122, 130, 134, 135, 169, 170, 172, 173, 175
Motivation 77, 131-133, 147, 185, 187
Naive 136, 137, 140, 143
Naturopathy 152
Neurolinguistic Programming 152
New Age 149, 150, 152
Non-focusing 76
Ownership 13, 53, 61, 67, 68, 73, 74, 78, 83, 85, 141, 162
Paradox Process 152
Past-Life Regression 152
Phineas Quimby 149
Phoenix Solution Outline 121

Power 11-13, 16, 17, 20-22, 27, 28, 30, 31, 33, 35, 37
43, 48, 53, 59, 66, 69, 73, 92, 100-102, 106, 118, 119, 135
143, 146, 147, 151, 153, 159, 170, 172, 19?
Preferences . . . . 55, 57, 18?
Primary Domino Thought . . 6, 89, 93-97, 99, 100, 102-105, 107-116
122, 123, 129, 150, 167, 170, 172, 17?
Principles of Psychotechnology . . . . 2?
Principle of Uncertainty 151
Privacy . . . . 17?
Problem Identification . . . . 71, 73, 79, 8?
Psychoimmunity . . . . 15?
Psychosynthesis . . . . 15?
Psychotechnology . . . . 7-8, 19-31, 148-153, 17?
Psychotronics . . . . 15?
Purpose 17, 90, 115, 116, 123, 132, 149, 161, 170, 173
180, 191, 193, 194
Quantum 131, 149-152, 154
Quantum Psychology 152
Rebirthing 152
Recontextualization 175-178
Reflective 82, 168
Regret 60, 61
Reiki 152
Resentment 15, 29, 45, 57, 60, 61, 187
Resourceful 168
Respectful 13, 168
Responsibility 13, 35, 39, 53, 58-61, 66, 68, 86, 121, 154, 157-
159, 163, 187
Responsible 35, 37, 38, 58-60, 108, 133, 168
Reticular Activating System 139
Revenge 60, 61
Righteousness 60, 61, 73
Rimplant 102, 103, 107
Shamanism 148, 149, 151, 152, 198
Shifting Contexts 99, 106, 113, 175